An

The music of the Temporalists

Many thanks to Ilinca Anghelescu and Adam Cole, who both were so kind as to proofread this book in 2015 and 2016, respectively.

Everything started on April 11th, 2008, just before noon. I was sitting in my easy chair enjoying a book, and, as is usual for fat people in their early fifties, after two or three pages my eyes started to spin the carousel of the same sentence, and in a little while I fell asleep. In the minutes that followed, my inner time must have gone astray, because the moment I woke up I found myself in the same room, at the same time of the same day – and yet my whole being was telling me loud and clear that more than two years had passed with that slumber. My head was throbbing and I was completely numb in my right hand. The effervescent aspirin I managed to dissolve in a glass of water brought me in front of the bathroom mirror, from whose silvery surface I was stared at by an apoplectic face with scary, crimson eyes. I was definitely sick, yet at the same time I felt an irrepressible urge to write. I could only compare the sensation with the compulsions that tormented the end of my childhood: for instance, each time I saw a wire stretched between two poles I would go crazy if I didn't roll my eyes while whistling four or five notes meant "to take me to the other side of the wire" – whatever that might have meant.

In the following days, I isolated myself in my study and, to my wife's amazement, I wrote a book. At the end of this intellectual effort I mustered around 250 written pages and, in the summer of the same year, I managed to rearrange or eliminate some of them, so that the story they contained would make as much sense as possible. Here and there I added new sentences, meant to clarify my actual point of view regarding the two apparently real and vivid years that the story covers.

In order to avoid, from this very outset, any misunderstandings that may occur in the future, I have to confess that I am a moderate music listener, of the sort that is interested more in the educated tickling of his sensations than in the critical competence that I might want to achieve. For instance, if while listening to the radio I come across a musical performance that really moves me, I won't rush to the computer to find out more about that musician's biography or recordings. Until that day of April, 2008, I had never pushed my pen to write anything about music, although since early childhood, a stable if not exceptional financial situation and my mother's unimaginative snobbism enabled me to reach a certain virtuosity as an amateur pianist. By the age of eighteen I was able to perform virtually any classical composition, in tempo and without missing a note – and that was the extent of it – unless I add in the fact that all the piano teachers who educated that diligent and submissive teenager noticed my peculiar talent for *tempi rubati*.

I was never interested in deepening my music theory expertise. Everything I know on the subject I found out in front of the keyboard, from my teachers, as they tried to explain to me the form of a particular composition, the musical genre to which that belonged or the terminology meant to define various compositional techniques and procedures. This is why I know so well the meaning of words such as countersubject, *ritornello* or hemiola. I was equally endowed by nature with a good memory and taught not to waste the building blocks of my education, by submitting myself to periodic recapitulations of the assimilated knowledge.

If from a musical point of view I can boast of the abilities just mentioned, psychology or, better said, the psychology of music perception represented to me, until recently, a completely alien domain. I used to consider that music was a cultural construct which, of course, makes use of our sensory competences – but, in order to understand it, these are not as important as the aesthetic conventions that were perpetuated or modified from one generation to the next. I thought that the conventions themselves, not the cognitive mechanisms that mediate this whole process, make us capable of judging a musical composition.

At this very moment I am almost fifty three years old and run the business inherited from my parents, as the owner of a small Parisian drugstore, ideally placed in the neighbourhood of a few office buildings crammed with stressed-out corporate employees who feed themselves on an impressive amount of wonder-pills that become more revolutionary and more expensive every day of the year. To put it in a nutshell: I am doing well enough to afford laziness.

Most of the time I can be found at home reading books or piano scores. The only nuisance of this lifestyle is to be found in the one hundred and two kilograms that define my silhouette no matter what or how much I eat.

All these being said, I rush to introduce into the memory of my computer the pages I wrote a few months ago. They definitely constitute the most bizarre thing I have experienced so far.

THE CONCERT

(Friday, April the 11th, 2008)

I dream (or am I dreaming?) that I am in a crowded concert hall. I would have said that it was a normal evening show if things weren't so different. The seats have cushions to stretch your legs upon, the stage looks like a small amphitheater, while in the orchestra that fills it I cannot find any recognizable musical instrument, although I see a wind and a string section. Before the lights start to fade away, I have just enough time to glimpse at the concertgoers seated around me. Their eyes are beautiful and their complexion grayish, like that of inveterate smokers or the second-day shadow on the chins of dark haired men. These people don't seem to belong to any human race that I know of. I mean, I couldn't place them on any of the five inhabited continents. Perhaps if I gathered all people with naturally astonished faces and let them crossbreed for a few generations I would get a race similar to this one.

I deeply regret that I have jotted down the impressions related to this concert now, after more than two years, when I could almost name the composers and the works performed. I can only try to recollect my first reactions, inevitably spoiled by the subsequent experiences. The orchestra, or should I say the octet, has no conductor but any of the eight instrumentalists is ideally placed to see his or her colleagues. While playing, they stare at each other and exchange cues by nodding their heads or raising their brows.

I assume that at first I was impressed by the overall sensation of a "job well done", by the apparent professionalism of the performers, although I was unable at that time to grasp the nature of their skills. Something seemed to be simply impeccable about their interpretation, both individually and as a chamber orchestra. The apperceptive background I was able to muster on that particular day made me believe that I was listening to a work written by a composer from the previous century, composed at any time between 1950 and 2008 – if I were to judge merely the sonorities.

What seemed really alien to me was the temporal universe through which all those microtonal pitches embraced the auditorium. I simply didn't know what to say, but I knew I liked that temporal texture the way I may like the inflections of a language I do not understand.

The music stops with a very approximated unison and the interpreters seem released from the intensity of the repeated exchanged glances I had noticed during the performance, only to redirect them to the public. No one claps hands. A few men from the first rows stand up and shake their heads vigorously, looking the performers straight in the eye, the same way, ages before, in my teens, I was stared at on the street by gay men who, I can only guess, found me attractive. Yet, a woman in the seat next to me does the same thing. All this ritual seems ridiculous. Most of the listeners are still seated, smiling and nodding their heads approvingly. While the members of the orchestra leave the stage, I have time to notice the beauty of the women and the caricature faces of the children who are quite adorable. They remind me of the comic books of my childhood, especially of the inquisitive faces of Jean Cézard's horses.

On the lowest level of the amphitheater stage a few men push in a new instrument which resembles a piano with a thousand keys, each one no thicker than a few millimeters. It looks like the keratin baleen of the whales my son used to draw when he was a child passionate about adventure books.

The "pianist" is an old woman who resembles the actress Ludivine Sagnier some forty years from now – if she gets fat and old the same way. I am anxious to see how that musical instrument will be played, and the restlessness is amplified by the orchestral introduction. Finally, the soloist produces the first sounds. The timbre resembles that of a hammerklavier, but I cannot imagine what kind of inner mechanism makes each finger attack produce only one sound, although several keys are pressed at the same time. I am listening to a kind of concerto for "piano" and chamber orchestra and I can tell that the style has changed, in comparison to the previous octet. I think that it was while I was listening to the dialogue between the soloist and the other instruments that I realized for the first time that, in this dream world, musical sounds are meant to serve an elaborated temporal fabric. I could neither read, perform or transcribe the bizarre rhythms I listened to, but there must be something magical about them since, while not understanding them, I find them so expressive. That was a memorably strange sensation. It reminds me of my first contact with Debussy's orchestral music, at Salle Pleyel. I was much too young for such an event. My mother had told me that I should be proud to be French, and I felt just that, falling in love for a few hours with a music that I was actually unable to comprehend.

In the small amphitheater, the music comes to a halt and the soloist repeats indefinitely the comical, muted ovation sequence. Meanwhile, the "whalebone" piano is taken away only to be replaced, to my astonishment, by a normal piano, on whose fallboard I can read: Olof Granfeldt. All of a sudden, I feel eyes on me from various places, and a small boy seated somewhere to my right points his finger in my direction until his mother stops him with a firm gesture. It seems that the lady on the stage is also looking for me through the obscure light of the concert hall. As the other instrumentalists have vanished backstage, I assume that there will be a kind of encore. Ha! It is a piano piece by Messiaen! I cannot tell which one, but I clearly recognize the composer.

It is hard for me to recollect now what kind of thoughts passed through my mind while the public followed the fingers of the player tapping the keys of that unacceptably out of tune Granfeldt piano. It's been quite a few years since then, yet I think that, while Messiaen's music became more and more a distant backdrop, my mind was still processing the first two compositions. They might have very well been the kind of music that Antoni Gaudi would have composed, had he not suffered from arthritis in his childhood, having thus the opportunity to approach a musical instrument and to become the composer to give shape, in sound and time – especially in time – to something resembling his hyperboloid architecture.

Unfortunately, that concert was the sole opportunity I had to listen to the music of these gray-faced men without having the slightest idea about its history, or indeed the very nature of the art their composers and music theorists were preoccupied with. Retrospectively, I would have liked to be exposed for a longer while, by means of a non mediated contact, to the iridescences of a music that is lofty, yet deeply human. It just so happened that in this case the music in question was not part of what we commonly name "the art of sound", but rather "the art of (musical) time".

As soon as the last chord of Messiaen's work dies out, to my great surprise, both the people in the audience and the interpreters who have returned from backstage turn their faces towards me, quite gawkishly, smiling and nodding their heads. It is now clear that I am living a strange dream (yes, I am!) in which I am no other than Olivier Messiaen. The lights are turned back on and the lady who played the piano beckons me onstage. Two young gentlemen, seated behind me and guarding a strange contraption, offer to escort me to the amphitheater through what I might call a flurry of ovational glances. As I reach my destination, the piano player gives me a hug and hails me with a comical accent, doubling all the "n"s in *biennvennu*. I manage to ask her if she speaks French, not realizing the sheer silliness of the question. The woman keeps silent while pulling me gently backstage, where a short man looks at me and smiles with his whole face.

– Welcome, he whispers. I will be your guide. You may call me what you wish, but my first French name was Jean-Philippe.

He must be in his late fifties, he is bald and his perching eyebrows make him look even more naturally astonished than the other people in the audience who, following a cue from the piano player, have started to applaud.

– It is you that the public acclaims, says Jean-Philippe, giving me a short nudge back onstage.

Fine, I say to myself, it is a dream in which I am *not* Olivier Messiaen. It's just me, reverencing in front of an audience clumsily clapping their hands. I am applauded for… nothing. If only I had performed my simple three ball trick. I hear Jean-Philippe shouting "Bravo!", a word that is taken over, with different accents, by two or three members of the public. There is a Texan one! The ovations die out slowly and I am guided through several hallways, over a few flights of stairs, and then along a dark corridor at whose end there is a door surrounded by some ventilation devices. Along with the piano player, Jean-Philippe and the two youngsters who had helped me onstage, I enter a forest that strikes me as odd because it looks cultivated like a garden. I can see signposts, picket fences and swept pathways.

Jean-Philippe starts talking to me. With a few intermissions, he will do just that, on a daily basis, for the next two years.

WHO THESE PEOPLE ARE
AND WHAT IS THAT THEY WANT FROM ME

J.-P.: If you are ever tempted to describe everything you see here, you will risk being definitively dubbed as a sci-fi author. What I suggest is that you learn as much as you can about our musical disciplines and, after you have returned home, write just about that, depending on how much you will be able to remember. Thus, the day the book we expect from you will be ready, the only risk you will have to face will be that the French publishing houses reject your manuscript on a normal, commercial basis. The musical publishing houses will send you their regrets and explain they don't publish fiction, while those who specialize in literature will say that they don't publish music theory. Yet... we rely on the probability that an editor of some influence will transform his personal frustration of having once abandoned the study of a musical instrument into a cautious "yes" jotted down on the first page of the manuscript.

Jean-Philippe speaks in long sentences, a manner of speech that was typical for the intellectuals of my grandfathers' generation. His French is so rigorous that at times I think he is reading something from a book. The accommodation week that was granted to me will soon come to an end. I had enough time to get familiar with most of the things my guide advises me *not* to write about.

J.-P.: If you find it absolutely necessary, you should sift the realities of our world through a Julesvernian filter. As a French gentleman who was once a little boy, that imaginative effort would fit you quite well, I believe. Don't hesitate to plunge back some 150 years, and you won't fail. Say that we use rivets instead of welding machines if you have to describe a bridge. Let the real version of your experience among us permeate only the pages dedicated to music.

That's how the short holiday in which I was encouraged to see, touch and ask came to an end. From that moment on, I would mostly open my ears wide open and learn.

J.-P.: In our world, the most sought after career is that of a psychologist. "Brain sciences specialist" is perhaps a better term, if not equally vague. It is precisely due to our discoveries in this field that we can now speak to each other in flesh and bone, although we both know that your actual body is now resting in your Parisian easy chair. Our experts made possible for your trip into our world to last only a few minutes back on the left shore of river Seine. They also helped me travel many times to the *Republique*, where I managed to learn the language and understand the French culture. Here is, briefly, what we can do with our brains there where you would invest impressive amounts of money and engineering, after a long trail of contractual agreements.

It was the very same day that Jean-Philippe explained to me how the recent history of his civilization is linked to the conquest of the human brain. No less than five generations of scholars swore that they would clear the virgin territories and chart the wide surface of the cortex onto which their predecessors ineptly wrote *hic sunt neurones*.

J.-P.: From this point of view, you folks are one step ahead, since you finished mapping of the human genome. We still dig the circumvolutive trenches of the human brain but, no matter the viewpoint, we are perfectly compatible. If we weren't the children of the same species, our meeting would have been pointless.

Jean-Philippe is married to Monique, who, of course, works in the most popular work field, doing something so specialised that, I was told, it would fit on the tip of a needle. The couple lives together with Yvonne, their sixteen-year-old daughter, who is also passionate about psychology and has been encouraged to follow in her mother's footsteps at a top university. The two women don't speak or understand French, but treat me affectionately. Their real names, in spite of my repeated efforts to find them out, remain unknown to me. Both of them giggled and tittered a whole evening while trying to make me pronounce different words in their language, including their real names. Jean-Philippe's vernacular is nothing that I could relate to any spoken idiom from our world. If I had to place it on our planet, I would put it in the mouth of some silent and as yet undiscovered species of fish. Sometimes, the accents and the temporal distribution of the syllables reminded me of Swedish, but I may be wrong. I was unable to grasp its sound or tonality. Some vowels last ludicrously long whereas others are short and percussive. I was able to discern groups of two successive accents, which is rare if not absent in our languages. Usually that happens in between two words, whereas in Jean-Philippe's language it may occur in the middle of a word.

The essential peculiarity of this strange language resides in the fact that the significance of the words is conveyed by the duration, stress and the prosodic function of each syllable of a word – and not by the series of vowels and consonants through which this word is being pronounced. A word like "amour" (which in their language is comprised of no less than twelve syllables) will always have the same pulsatory profile but, depending upon context and the specific emotion it has to express (platonic affection, patriotic fervor or love for the curls of a puppy) it may sound like "Bastille", "tarot" or "bijou". Jean-Philippe is of the opinion that, given my age, it will be impossible for me to understand their language as a result of an arbitrary effort – not even at a superficial level. He assures me that, after a short period, when my brain will have been sufficiently exposed to the sonority, or better said the *temporality* of his maternal language, they will find a solution for this shortcoming. The important thing is that, subconsciously, I develop an acute need to understand the meaning of the words floating into my ears.

The critical period in which their children learn to speak this peculiar language fluently coincides with a series of impressive neural modifications. The centre responsible for the recognition of the different pulsatory patterns that compose the words is more or less the same as that responsible for face recognition. Monique assures me, while Jean-Philippe translates, that this centre is placed in the heart of one of the most evolved cognitive capabilities of the human brain. More than that, due to the temporal configuration of their language, the speech centre is placed differently in the brains of my new friends.

I hope I was able to transcribe Monique's words accurately. It seems to me bizarre enough to put on paper things from a scientific domain so alien to me.

J.-P.: Whereas, from a genetic point of view, we are one hundred percent compatible, due to the paradigmatic difference of our notional utterance, at maturity, our brains differ significantly. Being myself one of the few *Temporalists* (yes, this was the term that my guide himself used) who managed to learn one of your languages, over the years I was annoyed with being the subject of a few hundred tests and analyses, but I also experienced the joy of meeting Monique in one of our advanced research laboratories. She claims that I possess one of the most enhanced brains in the Universe, and that is precisely due to the fact that I can express myself both in the alphabetical and the temporal modalities. These capacities are immensely enhanced, in my case, by the fact that, to boot, I am a musician trained in both systems: ours, that is mainly temporal, and the Western tradition, based on sonorous bidimensionality.

While recollecting Jean-Philippe's words, I realize that now it is perhaps the time to introduce the term by which I decided to define the representatives of the civilization that my guide belongs to. In just a short time, both he and his kind became to me "the Temporalists", and under this nickname, spontaneously launched by Jean-Philippe, I continued to represent my new friends during the two insomniac years that followed.

Returning to the Temporalist language, I was informed that the sounds that they articulate while speaking, while not randomly chosen, are still not subject to any fixed rules. As these sounds belong exclusively to an expressive, meta-linguistic, level of communication, they merely define contexts and convey emotional states. It was amusing for me to notice that, whenever Jean-Philippe and Monique had a domestic argument, their speech utilized more and more vowels and, as the ardor of their cues increased, I had the impression of a couple of quarreling Italians. Out of politeness, if not of pure curiosity, I wanted to pronounce the name of the beautiful and distinguished lady. Upon hearing my request, Jean-Philippe rolled his eyeballs and told me that, since I insist, her name is Thefourthfrenchrepublic.

– Ha, ha, I giggled, starting to understand. I noticed that the six syllables were pronounced weirdly, in the "Temporalist manner," the sound of which I was becoming accustomed to recognize. Well, if you call her by this name, will she know that you are looking for her?

He didn't call her by that name, but the moment the four of us gathered around the dinner table, Jean-Philippe produced a surprising feat by speaking at the same time both to me and to the two women. The bizarre accents with which he maltreated the French language made me more attentive to his words, whereas for the wife and daughter – so I was told afterwards – the only strange things were the sounds of the French language by which Jean-Philippe managed to convey the pulsatory patterns while asking them for more boiled sinews and simultaneously telling me that he was starving.

When they speak normally, the shortest sounds last about one tenth of a second. If they hurry, the length of the syllables become more uniform, nearing isochronicity and making me wonder how these people understand each other. That is where the vowels and consonants they spontaneously choose to use have a big role to play. One day I took a wrong underground train and sat near two young French teenagers who were definitely speaking the language of the encyclopedists, yet I was unable to understand most of the words. They didn't seem to have a problem understanding one another.

The modern Temporalist alphabet uses a series of graphic symbols that correspond to the different lengths of the syllables. In fact, these lengths are mostly theoretical, as the language is a living body and may distance itself from the written convention to places as unchartable as the slang of the two teenagers when compared to the pronunciation one may still hear from the lips of the old actors of the French Comedy. The fact that there is a Temporalist alphabet helped me immensely. While spending hundreds of hours in their musical libraries, I was able to identify the names of the composers and interpreters listed in the catalogues.

I wrote these few paragraphs about the language and writing of my friends only to show in the following pages that the way these people conceived their music is evidently linked to the temporal nature of their notional communication. To give just an example, the duration both of the syllables and of the musical notes ranges between about 100 and 1500 milliseconds. Also, during the period considered by the Temporalists to be their Classical era, the structures that we may associate with our idea of musical motifs were comprised of groups of 7-8 notes – precisely the number of syllables most Temporalist words are composed of. The similarities go on.

One morning, Yvonne stormed into the living room all aglow, showing us her rain-soaked clothes. Upon listening to her, Jean-Philippe started to smile and announced me that we shall all move to the kitchen "because outside it pours down with sufficiently big raindrops". I had no reason to protest, given the fact that my guide had just replenished my glass of wine – in fact an alcoholic beverage no stronger than 12-13%, with a taste resembling that of the plum wine one may drink in some of the Korean restaurants scattered throughout Paris. Monique was already in the kitchen, happily stomping the floor while clearing into in a large basket all the things left on the table. Jean-Philippe popped in, carrying a kind of hose which he fit into a hole in the ceiling. At the other end of the hose there was a funnel covered with a large cork made of some dark felt. Yvonne started handing out paper sheets and writing tools. They suggested I bring for myself the flask of wine that was left in the living room.

The oldest Temporalist family game goes like this: on the roof of every old house there is a metallic slab fitted with several small plates that sound like a *bloc chinois*. Depending on where the plates are hit by the raindrops, the sound they produce can last longer or shorter. All the vibrations are taken over by the metallic slab and conveyed through a pipe, down to a hole in the kitchen (or dining room) ceiling. As we already know, Jean-Philippe's playground is located in the kitchen. Whenever it rains with large drops – which is a rare occurrence in this forested area – families gather around the contraption, set up the amplifiers and, removing the corks from the funnels, listen attentively to the random messages of the rain. Soon enough, the Temporalist mind starts to fathom words the same way our grandmothers saw handsome officers, broken hearts and secret romances in coffee dregs. The rain patter is seen by them as a generous dictionary that scatters around not only infinitive verbs and nominative nouns, but also past or future progressives and articulated forms. As all Temporalists are very good at deciphering these rain whisperings, the game unfurls at a lively pace, every player claiming a word out of a long series, but only if all participants agree that the respective word was clearly heard. Thus, after Jean-Philippe's first choice, Monique and Yvonne picked their own words, and the game went around the room nine more times until the rain was silenced with the help of the felt cork. The second part of the game is a kind of word domino in which the first word picked is placed on the table, the next alongside it etc., so that in the end the resulted dadaist sentence must be grammatically correct. The players with a good memory already know the other (in our case) 29 words and who exactly is to place them on the table, so that they will have an edge during the negotiations. The idea is that anyone can place a word in front or at the end of the words already displayed. If two players compete for the same place in the domino, the third decides the winner. In such situations, the contenders will accept the burden of having to declare which word (or words) they are about to use. If there are too many words, the "referee" will be tempted to give an advantage to the player who has fewer words to add, but there are cases where the referee will let the player with more words win if his or her words create an advantage for the referee himself. If all players intend to add words in the same place, the winner is the player who can align the most words at once. Finally, if the number of words to be placed in the same spot are the same for each player, any negotiation or alliance is accepted, even unplayed words transactions – until the deadlock is overcome. In most cases, after each player has placed the first four or five words of his own on the table, the sentence gets stuck, in which case, if the rain is still falling, the felt cork is removed one more time from the amplifier and the first word that may unlock the phrase is added to the domino. If the rain has stopped, there is always a small purse containing leftover words from previous games. Thus, the game can go on. The winner is the first player who gets rid of his ten words while the loser is the Temporalist who has placed the fewest words on the table. In the end, all unused words are introduced into the purse to be used at the next rainfall. The resulting phrase, usually composed of 20-25 words, is copied into a special notebook. My friends own such a notebook that is over 200 years old, inherited from Monique's family branch.

J.-P.: The eeriest thing is that the texts you can read here have little resemblance to the phrases jotted down by our parents, while the latter are different in comparison to our own sentences. If you ignore the outdated words, the only conclusion one can draw is that in the past it rained differently.

Oh, Jean-Philippe, I know that you would give me a good telling off if you found out that I wasted a few pages to describe the rain game. No week has passed in the two years that I spent among Temporalists without my dear friend reminding me that in my book-to-be I should confine my subject to the basics of their musical theory that he, along with a scholar whom I will introduce later, has so patiently explained to me.

J.-P.: You will know that you failed in your mission if, by entering a bookstore, library or used books shop, you will find your creation placed on the science fiction shelf. If it will be placed in the "memoirs" section, you have done a mediocre job, whereas, if you will have known how to meet our highest expectations, you will find the book listed among the musicology works. The choice is yours.

My friends laughed out loud whenever I tried to pronounce their names, and yet a similar thing happened when Monique or Yvonne wanted to call me. I knew they were looking for me from the intensity of their shout, always composed of two syllables, the last one invariably keeping the "r" from André. I was thus called, in the first week, by many names: Norah, Oirée, Piron or, unbelievably, Maigret. Any attempt from my part to make the two women concentrate on the sounds of my name – Aaan-dré – failed in a comical mixture of approximations. When she was five years old, my daughter had her musical ear tested. I would press the piano keys at random and ask her to sing along the respective pitches, in her register, and she would do just that with her trombone-like voice. Well, even my ungifted daughter managed to sing some of the sounds perfectly in tune. The two women were totally unable to approximate the sound of my name. Jean-Philippe had surpassed this both cultural and perceptual handicap some forty years before, when his brain was "optimized" to have a functional configuration similar to our brains. If I got it right from Monique, our main speech centre is located somewhere in the left hemisphere, behind the temple. In Temporalists, things are more complicated because notional communication activates several regions of the cortex. As I have already mentioned, in order to recognize different pulsatory patterns, a Temporalist individual uses an area of the brain that is also responsible for facial recognition. When they speak, several areas of their brains are activated. At some point Monique mapped for me all these details and I tried to represent them following Jean-Philippe's approximate translation – he was not familiar with the French terms used to describe human brain anatomy. I was surprised to find out that professional musicians in both worlds develop in time certain anatomical modifications of the brain. Music seems to be one of the few human activities that can trigger such an evolution.

I asked Jean-Philippe how come that he eventually managed to activate his capacity to recompose words and notions from the sonorous representations of vibrating air particles. He replied that the question was posed to him many times and that the best analogy he was able to make for his compatriots became available the moment some of his colleagues managed to replicate on Temporalist soil the technology by which we make those amazing stereovisual images. Paradoxically, if you are not aware of what they represent, the more you focus on their surface, the more you distance yourself from their graphical conundrum. All it takes is a moment of relaxation, in which the tormented eyes look for a resting point somewhere at the horizon, for a 3D contour to emerge from the hitherto fuzzy picture. From the moment Jean-Philippe managed for the first time to coordinate the motion of his lips in accordance with the spoken sounds, and not with the duration of the syllables, everything else became a matter of practice. In order to achieve the capacity to speak and understand French language at an acceptable level, he needed no less than twenty years. The cells composing his body refreshed several times during this period, while his brain became an object of scientific research.

From my point of view, it seemed unbelievable for one to hear combinations or vowels and consonants without being able to discern them beyond a superficial level. The whole story ceased to seem so extraordinary the moment I remembered the gray winter days when my mother tried to cheer me up with stories from her interbellum childhood spent with her family in Oloron-Sainte-Marie. During those years, almost every household owned at least four sheep, given in care to the shepherds of the Pyrenees Mountains, who kept them up in the pastures. There were no formal contracts except for a verbal agreement, always respected by both parties. At the beginning of every spring break all the small farms were visited by an old shepherd who would take over the wintered sheep and gather them on the large common at the southern outskirts of the town. Before noon, the place would be crowded with thousands of ewes kept together with some mobile fences and a few dozen furry Pyrenee dogs. The next morning, all these animals were supposed to start their journey to the alpine pastures, in groups of up to 300 sheep, led by the shepherds and their families. The old man was responsible with the sorting and the allotment of the livestock. It was not permitted for animals taken from one farm to be placed in the same flock. Thus, no one risked losing all the animals due to any of the possible misfortunes. My mother used to tell me that during that unique day of the year, the sheep owners would witness an amazing performance: the old shepherd would look at each and every sheep, telling in a loud voice from whose house it was taken and then distributing it to one of the younger shepherds. He would do that writing down the data in a kind of ledger. As there were thousands of sheep, out of which quite a few were seen by the shepherd for the first time in his life, the locals couldn't hide their amazement. To them, all sheep looked the same. Perhaps a few were able to recognize their own animals in those large flocks that were about to head to the pastures near Issor and Escot. Despite all that, before sunset all the sheep would be distributed as agreed. The same demonstration would take place in reverse order during the last days of autumn, when the old shepherd would return the animals to their respective owners – needless to say, making no mistake.

For Temporalist ears, the sounds we produce while speaking are as many sheep, mixed together in the flock of their own indistinctness. Similarly, the temporal filigree of Temporalist speech remained for me an intangible ability.

A short time after I became convinced that my life among Temporalists could not be just a dream, I asked Jean-Philippe why they picked me to experience this mental journey into their world. Here is what he replied:

J.-P.: Please do not feel diminished in any way, but we were simply looking for a person with a good memory, capable to epitomize in detail, during the critical four-five day period that follows the return to his or her initial life, the music theory of a human civilization that is so dissimilar in comparison to yours. The fact that you are an experienced amateur pianist constituted an important trump card for choosing you from among other candidates, as was the orderly fashion in which you keep the objects in your study. Finally, we knew that you were in every other respect a citizen in good standing of the French Republic, and that is why we hope that you won't be considered so easily a mere lunatic the moment you will try to publish the book on our music and claim that you have annotated in it a de facto experience. To be frank, there were those that regretted the fact that we were not able to find someone with your qualities who also had an extended expertise in cognitive psychology. This shortcoming will be soon taken care of by a professor that you are about to meet who spent the last two years seeking for a method by which our music theory could be explained to practically anyone. If you ask me, I think that if in your stead we had brought a full-fledged psychologist, he or she would have pestered us with dozens of meta-musical questions and would have projected all his or her elaborate preconceptions upon our wonderful art. A complete failure, André. I can only imagine that a similar failure would have been my specialization in European music, had I had my wife's training. Well, you should know that before I chose you, I chose the French culture. I managed to persuade my colleagues that yours is the only civilization that is both sufficiently advanced and apparently not so obsessed with

17

"being right" all the time. As a general state of mind... but we shall talk about this subject in the years to come.

The subject was indeed put again on the table, in a surprising context.

J.-P.: If we only consider the chronology of our recent histories, the evolution of our civilizations is quite similar. By the outset of your industrial revolution, in this world the first manifestos and manifestations of our "Brain Revolution" began to storm the minds of our forefathers. In the following two centuries, both civilizations developed a consistent middle class, composed there mainly of entrepreneurs, engineers, lawyers and various specialists – and here of the representatives of the many branches of the brain sciences. There are chemists and doctors here as well, but we should add to their respective titles prefixes such as "psycho-" or "neuro-". As you may have observed, our level of comfort is no better than that of the average French bourgeoisie in mid 19th Century. We do not have speedy cars, fancy highways or, indeed, your personal computers. Yet our brains, optimized through various methods, can achieve things that you and your technology won't be able to conceive any time soon. Once the results of our Revolution became commonplace, arts too began to be studied as psychophysical realities, as a sum of cognitive processes. The new generations were discouraged from discovering by themselves the way they react emotionally and intellectually to our classical music. Fortunately, my parents, who were still resisting this tendency, allowed me to become an empirical music lover. Thus I first had the chance to hierarchize my likes and dislikes for myself, by composers and styles, and I was only later introduced to the practical and theoretical aspects of this art. Luckily enough, the Brain Revolution has never been a thorough success in our musical institutions. The schoolbooks our students use today are still updated variants of the old treatises, written long ago, when the music itself was surpassing in quality. There are of course musicians who blame this conservatism and try to advocate the idea that today the Brain Revolution is the natural course for musical creativity. We respect their opinion and let them argue between themselves the countless theories they produce every day of the year. Add to that the fact that these scholars always have the necessary resources, as they ally themselves with the scientists with whom they share a common language. If you want, they constitute our avant-garde, very much silenced these days because our concert-goers started to genuinely enjoy European music. Let me explain this: about forty years ago, when we managed to import from your countries the first Tonal Harmony principles, our musicians started to realize the error of considering the sonorous dimension of music a mere decoration, meant

18

to subserve the temporal plot of any given musical composition. We were literally stunned to discover the sheer complexity of the aesthetic rules that verticalize and, may I say, horizontalize in your music a simplified system of twelve equally distanced pitches. Our psychologists were unable to refrain themselves from asking for the Psychophysics treatises on whose basis the Harmony or Counterpoint schoolbooks were written. Even if those existed, you have to understand that we can only import from your world the information that an optimized brain can memorize. As such, I have brought from Paris a mind that was imbued with French language and culture, but could not bring a freshly baked baguette to present my wife with. Therefore, the claim from our scholars that someone be sent to Europe in order to memorize a book on tonal music perception was deservedly considered a waste of resources and consequently discarded. It was only later that the same scholars were surprised to find out from people like me that the Tonal Harmony schoolbooks were not written "on the basis" of any kind of perceptual psychology compendia, since they are the result of a sustained common effort that established conventions and laws of an impressionist, aesthetic nature, often times placed against the grain of any apparent scientific basis. As soon as the news spread, there were many voices noticing the amazing similarities between the two musical worlds: we also have a sophisticated system for the theoretical representation of music that created a consistent body of masterpieces *before* the outbreak of the Brain Revolution. This is, my dear friend, the similarity that unites our musical cultures.

After this dissertation, I dared to ask my guide something that had been nagging at me for some time: namely why, since all "imports" from my world are purely mental, I am sitting in the same room with him, how I eat, drink and converse with a gentleman who has just told me twenty odd times that I am definitely *not* dreaming.

J.-P.: Well… perhaps this moment is as good as any other. All that you have to do is trust me and look at your hands.

Not knowing what to believe, I did just that – only to plunge myself into a state of shock after noticing that my fingers… were not mine! Up to that moment I was so excited by the novelty of the world into which I had been "imported" that I was completely unaware of the actual state of my body. Now I had Temporalist, grayish fingernails and a small scar at the basis of my left thumb. My skin also displayed my friends' cinder pigmentation, while my eyes seemed to have been cured of nearsightedness. I shouted that I wanted to see my face immediately and Jean-Philippe hurried to bring me a purse mirror, in which I was able to see the caricatural countenance of a chubby Temporalist who, putting aside the racial differences, looked quite similar to my real self.

J.-P.: The owner of your... this body asks you to take good care of it during the few minutes in which his mind will be in Paris, and especially during the two years in which you will use it in our world. Oh! He insists on you doing your best to keep it slim. You know... his wife is saddened enough by the volunteer status of her spouse. Now you know why you won't be able to take back with you anything except your memories and why it is so important for us to focus on one sole subject, that is, music.

Jean-Philippe told me that the Tonal Harmony principles were consequently monopolized by those who later were to become their specialists in pitch perception. They rejoiced to find out that the whole chromatic scale may be deduced from the natural resonance of a fundamental sound. My friend was unsuccessful in trying to show that explaining European musical tradition on the basis of this physical phenomenon is like trying to quantify a spiritist séance. Unfortunately, in the years this debate was gaining momentum, the only European music Temporalists at large were able to listen to was a series of melodies ineptly sung (to say the least) by their emissaries returned from either shore of the Atlantic Ocean. Not even the first Temporalist replica of a European keyboard put the debate on the right path, because concertgoers were not used to following harmonic progressions, while their first piano players did not surpass the technical skills of a mediocre second grade child attending the piano classes at our Ecole Normale de Musique on the Malesherbes Boulevard. It was only a later development that the lady I had listened to performing the Messiaen composition managed to equate the virtuosity of a professional pianist and "the music of sounds", as our art is called there, became a trendy thing, thus triggering more resources for the import of the music we listen to in our concert halls or whenever we plug the iPod pads into our auricular orifices. By the time I stepped down into their world, things were just starting to budge, and their psychologists still studied the Tonal Harmony schoolbooks as if these were a collection of laws and axioms – not realizing that the more immutable these were regarded to be, the more distanced they actually were from the tradition that made them possible.

As one of his assigned tasks was to import from the French speaking countries every valuable idea regarding pitch systems, Jean-Philippe realized that it would be interesting that we too benefit from the things that Temporalists were able to export – from a musical point of view. Given their own experience with this kind of cultural interchange, Jean-Philippe hoped to avoid placing their musical tradition in the hands of some logical positivism or cognitive musicology Cerberuses, who would probably only repeat the mistake of protecting the theory of an aesthetic construction as a set of rules independent from the lively tradition that made the rules possible in the first place. My friend's recommendation was followed by a long period of slow moving debates and assessments, the debacle being triggered by a musicologist who wrote an article stating that, for their future generations, the benefit of such an endeavour would be incalculable. In time, the fundamental data of their musical tradition, once placed in the hands of Western musicians, could shape "another Temporalist musical tradition".

J.-P.: As soon as I read that article, I started to frisk like a puppy and conveyed to the author my warmest thanks. Imagine, André, what this man had said... it is as if a music-loving God had cloned humankind just before the Renaissance, one Planet Earth remaining that which we both know, while the other was allowed to develop an alternative history. People would marry different spouses, other children of the same cultures would be born and, as a consequence, European music would have developed differently, within the frame of the same tradition. There would have been perhaps another kind of Baroque followed by other trends and composers who – God knows what kind of music they would have created. Wouldn't it be great if we could observe the bifurcated evolution of a given tradition? But you know so well the wonders the old European instruments and tuning system produced once put in the hands of the Afro-Americans about a century ago. We expect something similar to happen a few generations after you have planted the first seed of our culture in the heart of the Western musical culture.

(Summer of 2008)
It was, I think, the very same day that Jean-Philippe explained to me what he meant when he said that French culture was spared "the obsession of being right". My guide had, of course, music in mind when he pronounced these words, and particularly what he used to call "the last bastion of analytical intellectualism". I have to admit that his argument was a little bit over my head, and consequently I fear to alter it by reproducing it here, from memory. I remember him stating that all stylistic leaps that European music ever witnessed were not the consequence of the fact that the older generations "were wrong" while the younger generations "were right". The same way, Jean-Philippe continued, the fact that no new pitch system ever replaced the twelve tone system is no proof that our forefathers "were right".

I jot down this note in the summer of 2008, trying to gather the unfinished ideas I took down during the few days in which I completed this book. I now realize how right Jean-Philippe was when he advised me to write "everything" down in the very first days after my return from the Temporalist world. My very reliable memory started to fail me, and I wonder now how it was possible for me to recollect the body of ideas that Jean-Philippe flooded me with at the very beginning of my musical journey. Two years later, when the moment arrived for us to say farewell, he warned me that I would bring to Paris a brain that was modified not only by the novel extra-European experience, but also by their experts in cortical optimization, which would make me feel the urge to write as a compulsion similar to that of a smoker who lights his tenth morning cigarette, although every cell of his or her body shouts out loud that the first nine were quite enough to temporarily quench the urge.

J.-P.: Perhaps it would have been easier for us to store into your memory our musical theory schoolbooks in my French translation and, once returned home, ask you to transcribe them word by word. The problem is that the way we relate to the temporal dimension of communication differs so much in the two worlds that no one would know what to do with those schoolbooks. However, I had a similar experience... After learning your language, my musical background qualified me to become the first representative of my civilization to appropriate the concepts of the musical trove which Western culture had gathered in the past 500 years. As to us the most amazing thing was your acquired ability to work with sounds, the first thing I did the day I started this adventure was to access the musical libraries of Paris and read all the available Tonal Harmony treatises. I remember well that the first such book was Salomon Jadassohn's *Harmonielehre*, in French translation. In the evenings, after hours of intellectual boggling in which I would learn the meaning of terms such as major and minor chords, inversions, cadences and modulations, I would return to the *garconnière* of the old lady whose body I was wearing at that time and switch on the FM receiver, always set on Radio Classique, trying to link in the slightest possible way the Haydn quartette just being aired to the body of information that I had crammed into my mind during that day. A total fiasco. I was unable to understand how it was possible to read a book on wine-making without being able to apply it once the grapes are ripe. Everything changed, of course, the day I decided to see how French children learn Harmony, and I saw them taking solfeggio classes and learning to play a musical instrument, thus educating and enhancing their perceptual capabilities. "So European musicians too have another kind of brain," I said to myself, suddenly understanding everything. Thus, a fraction of Madame Richaume's next pension distribution was converted into the cheapest CASIO piano keyboard I could find and as such I set out the long journey of musical professionalization at whose end I was able to name the chords I would hear or represent mentally the musical notes I would see written in the scores. This is why, my dear friend, we shall encourage you to describe the way our music is taught in schools – or else your compatriots will face the same bewilderment I experienced while wearing the skirts of an old lady. I still wonder what her distant relatives might have thought, had they discovered that this well-mannered and unobtrusive person had spent the last years of her life, sometimes ten hours a day, reading the most arid books on musical theory.

It seems that this proportion – a few minutes in the original environment versus about two years in the destination world – represents the optimum option for resource spending (I never understood what these Temporalist "resources" really represented).

Jean-Philippe was sent on this kind of lengthy trips several times, visiting approximately the same European years, thus witnessing quite a few paradoxical experiences: at some point he sat in the reading hall of *Bibliothèque Musicale Gustav Mahler* three desks away from Madame Richaume, who was engrossed in the study of Vincent d'Indy's Harmony exercises. One trip before, Jean-Philippe had attended for the third (and last) time the modest interment of the old lady in the *Division israelite* of the Montparnasse cemetery, in whose ground the very author of the *Poèmes des rivages* rested his bones.

– But weren't you curious at all to have an incognito conversation with yourself? I questioned Jean-Philippe.

He told me that he would have loved to approach one of his younger former avatars, or even an older one, but, in the name of God, not the old lady avidly reading some thick music theory tomes!

J.-P.: Yet I am glad I never saw my first avatar. A thirty-two-year-old autistic man who strived to learn French by himself.

The first word Jean-Philippe ever pronounced was "Nathalie". He had heard it a thousand times coming from the open windows of the second floor teenager who wished to see herself dead – but not before playing on and on the same single record that would never wear off. The parents of the autistic man were stunned to hear their son murmuring quite clearly this girl's name. During this thirty two years of equanimous sadness, they were unable to make him utter anything but some indistinct mumbles.

(Summer of 2008)
Jean-Philippe does not only have a wonderful command of the French language, but he is also a great storyteller. It is no wonder that he knows so many things, since his brain has recorded the life of a 120-year-old man, of which only 57 years were spent in the Temporalist world. The remaining years

added up from his many eight-season trips span the period between 1965 and 2007. Thus, the main body of his mental experience was shaped in Paris.

It has been several hours since I started to write this account, and I have only recollected the first Temporalist experiences, including the first "lectures" delivered to me by Jean-Philippe. Yet, the mission of this book is different... I should soon start describing the theory that organizes their strange musical art. But there is still time. After all, it has only been a few hours since I was kissing a blushing Yvonne on the cheek, though her father had reassured her that such gestures are acceptable in Paris, between two old friends.

J.-P.: After having returned Madame Richaume's body to its rightful owner, I started to explain to my compatriots the "real life" of the tonal system, showing the ways in which it is based on practice and perceptual enhancement, both within the frame of a vast tradition. As soon as I did that, I was assailed with dozens of funny, if inept questions, such as "What is the speciality of the psychologists who invented the concept of dissonance?", "Has the chromatic modulation been discovered by German psychologists?", "In which period composers were first allowed to use it?", "How dared Debussy spurn the perceptual laws so painstakingly established by the psychologists of the previous centuries?!". Dear André, it seems that the more we understand our brain, the more space human stupidity finds to manifest. You are still using a small percentage of your intellect, to say nothing of the fact that you still didn't solve the shameful sleep problem. You waste one third of your lives just kicking around like hibernating bears. Well, under these circumstances, I fear that the specialists from tangential disciplines such as cognitive musicology, perceptual psychology or even bar-rhythmical fanatics will skin you alive... Perhaps you will have your share of stupid questions.

In the two years that followed, Jean-Philippe provided me with a fistful of advice meant to pre-empt such a prospective experience. Ideally, by reading this book, musicians should find out that they need to know more about temporal perception, and psychologists that they have to learn some music theory. As for those who are familiar with both domains – and those who generally belong to that category of people "obsessed to be right" that Jean-Philippe had told me about – I was advised to tell them the tightrope parable...

The tightrope parable

Within an experiment designed in accordance with the strictest academic rules, one thousand subjects, picked up from a world in which acrobatics had not yet been invented, were asked to stride barefoot across the whole length of a tightrope placed one foot over the ground, in between two trees situated twenty yards apart. At the end of the experiment, the following facts were recorded: tightrope walking is possible but not sustainable in humans, as most subjects fell down after the first two to four paces.

Jean-Philippe explained that these kind of experiments constitute the raw material for systematic musicology adepts. They genuinely allow themselves to be influenced by the quantified results coming from experimental psychology, often times transferring its data to the ever surprising world of "optimized brains" – to use Jean-Philippe's term. Such a brain was, I assume, that of the old shepherd of the Pyrenees who, if we go by the results of the scholarly study "Mnemonic capacity of human brain in relation to the ovine facies", is a freak. (*I wrote the last paragraph today, July 8th, 2008, at Dieppe, after a nauseating argument with a music loving engineer who, upon seeing me proofreading these pages, asked me bluntly: "Actually, what do you do for a living?"*).

It is my understanding that Jean-Philippe tried not to interfere with our world at all. Over the years, my guide inhabited the bodies of an autistic man, a deaf and mute teenager, and several sulky old people with severe mental impairments such as Alzheimer disease.

A common recurrence in our music-related dialogues was the topic of our temporal framework: the bar-rhythmical system. Jean-Philippe explained to me that in their world, too, there is a kind of repetitive music (he even called it quasi-minimalist) that is generally embraced by teenagers who don't know how to entertain themselves during the excited boredom of the amorous prelude. In his opinion, in both our worlds, the difference between bad repetitive music and good repetitive music is not big enough – and that explains, in Jean-Philippe's view, the little interest older Temporalists paid to this kind of music.

J.-P.: Before understanding the way I was supposed to follow the sonorous fabric of your music, I wondered what European listeners found so interesting in those tedious, at times "square" rhythms that permeate most music written on your five line staves. My brain, so much used to perceive sounds as the background and temporal discretisation as the foreground, did not help me understand your interest in those musical compositions made of two or three rhythmical values, usually the beat and one or two smaller values. Conversely, I can only imagine that you will be equally disappointed by the sonorous dimension of our music. In our case, the absence of sound won't make a well known composition unrecognizable, the same way an isochronal arrangement of the chords that any Brahms symphony starts with won't make your concertgoers wonder what they are listening to. I am envious of the future generations who in either world will be able to master both sonorous and temporal Harmony.

I have no idea whether placing these section titles here and there is a good thing to do. My brain is flash-flooded by so many ideas at once that I find it hard to focus on one subject at a time. In the previous chapter I managed to keep with the announced topic, but will I be able to do the same here? I had better be, since outside the sun is setting and I have so far been unable to introduce the main topic of this book: Temporalist music theory.

At the end of my accommodation week, during an evening that seemed to instill the first signs of routine in the heart of my new life, Jean-Philippe invited me to join him for "a long walk to the house of a venerable psychologist, the only person able to present me with some important knowledge". The timing couldn't have been worse, as I felt unusually sleepy and I was just about to call it a day and go to bed in "my" room that once belonged to Jean-Philippe's son. I had had enough time during that week to notice that, whenever I said that I should go to bed, the two beautiful women couldn't refrain from making a grimace or exchanging petrified looks, as if I were asking for a bucket into which to empty the content of my stomach. A few months would pass before I found out that, within the Temporalist mores, sleep is associated to breast-feeding, both the mother and the newborn relishing this senseless waste of time under the protection of a long established tradition. Sleep is also tolerated for very old or very ill persons. Everyone else, from the three year old bantling to the oldest Temporalist, eats the leaves of a plant (tea, salad, broth etc.) that successfully eliminates our natural need for sleep. As the Temporalist name of this plant crams no less than twenty one syllables, outlining a temporal profile that I wouldn't dare to explain, I chose to name it "tota": the coca leaf of the Temporalist world.

Upon realizing that my intentions were real, Jean-Philippe entered the kitchen whence he returned carrying a bowl of cold tea, both wishing me good night and, very much to my amazement, telling me that he would be outside the house, waiting for me. I gulped the contents of the bowl and, as I was about to climb into bed, I suddenly experienced a feeling that I always associated with childhood, and particularly to those days when I would be summoned to get my "afternoon slumber" in the middle of the most compelling game of button football. I soon realized that I was experiencing the effects of the scalded tota leaves, enhanced by a strange feeling of acute affection that projected on the screen of my consciousness these two words: "old friend". I can only compare it to the sensation I was engulfed by some thirteen years ago, when a South-American friend offered me, for the first time in my life, a cup of *yerba-maté*, prepared in a hollowed pumpkin and served with a genuine silver *bombilla*.

Outside, Jean-Philippe was loading into a kind of gig various bottles, packed food, clothes, blankets and writing tools. In between the wheels there was a spring mechanism, similar to those used for the manufacture of wind-up mice. I was soon to find out that this chaise, approximately two meters long by one meter wide, is the main Temporalist vehicle, well suited for a world in which people are not used to covering long distances unless it becomes an absolute exigency. The mechanism placed above the axle was meant to store the energy necessary for the uphill segments of the road. Jean-Philippe told me that our itinerary would take us across a mostly flat terrain, and that we should be on our way at dawn, just after the moment when insects go to sleep.

(Summer of 2008)
I have just crossed out the pages in which I had depicted nature, roads and the few Temporalists we met along the way during the forty-odd hours in which, harnessed to the gig like a pair of horses, we covered the distance that separated us from the house of the "venerable psychologist". I only left in the ideas by which Jean-Philippe wanted to prepare me for the imminent meeting with Herr Schmidt etc.

The Temporalist conclave that initially planned to "import" me had reached the conclusion that their music theory is too abstract for a man who was not capable to perform even the simplest musical structures written in their peculiar notation. Someone ought to present me with the basic cognitive mechanisms upon which initially the whole Temporal Harmony was empirically built up. In other words, there was a complex music theory that was conceived before the Brain Revolution, and a cognitive approach to it, formulated after the Revolution, by the many psycho-musicians of the modern Temporalist society. The main problem was that the terminology, the depth and scope of the expertise, and the complexity of the perceptual phenomena explaining the eco-logical framework of Temporal Harmony could only bewilder a poor French gentleman like me who, if not attentive enough, could mistake psychology for psychoanalysis and both for psychiatry. The solution to this dilemma was found in the person of Dr. Schmelzig etc., an eighty-odd year-old celebrity who had spent no less than 102 years in our Western hemisphere, where he studied the German, Dutch and English-speaking civilizations. He was fluent in all these languages plus a Flemish dialect and cherished a visceral disdain for anything French.

He had just completed a long account of his last two-year trip across the United States, where he successfully "parasyted" the bodies of some gaga scholars who were still granted access to academic citadels such as the Massachusetts Institute of Technology or the Haskins Laboratories of Connecticut. The Temporalist octogenarian was known for his custom of pouring boiled water over the tota leaves a moment before each two year long trip, only to find the tea perfectly infused after the few minutes in which his mind had scoured our universities.

The American sojourn had been a deviation from his current activities, made entirely "in my honor". His assignment was to see how their temporal perception psychology could be formulated using the rudimentary terminology of a civilization that had not experienced a Brain Revolution and, further on, how this translation could be simplified so that its meaning be comprehended "by the brains of a man whose ancestors only lived to pass on sophisticated food recipes and to write thick novels about how they have sex, from dusk to dawn". These were the precise words Professor Schönwald etc. used when he communicated to my guide that he would be honored to host us in his house for a prolonged visit.

When, overwhelmed by this bout of frankness, Jean-Philippe asked him what was the "original sin" that, in his illustrious eyes, the French people committed, Doktor Schindler etc., who had lived several times through the Second World War both in London and in Bavaria, replied: "The German and English cultures are like the two hemispheres of the same brain, unfortunately short-circuited by the French epilepsy!". I was soon to discover that one of the reasons Jean-Philippe accompanied me on this visit was to encourage me not to lose my sense of humour. In addition, he would translate any English word I wouldn't understand. Not that they were too many, as my English is quite good – I suppose, since I am able to follow the BBC World Service broadcasts. Finally, Jean-Philippe would remain my first adviser as far as music theory was concerned, since Mr. Schnabel etc. declined his competence over this domain, although he benefited from a solid musical education up to his late childhood.

Notwithstanding magister Schönbrunn's etc. behavioral deficiencies, Jean-Philippe assured me that our meeting would be entirely constructive, given the cumulated age of the character – almost two centuries – and his quality of having been the beneficiary of so many Temporalist "resources", given to him for pure merit.

J.-P.: Psychologists have always benefitted from this point of view.

I remember the morning I saw a cultivated strip of land for the first time on Temporalist soil. We had just exited that endless forest and were enjoying the light from a sun no different from the one I greet from the balcony of my Parisian apartment. The tota tea effects didn't seem to vanish as I tried to follow each and every word uttered by the other "mule", who had kept talking all through the previous night.

J.-P.: You should never forget that the music theory that you will start to learn tomorrow is a version that was custom-designed to meet your understanding. It perhaps best resembles the tempered tuning system of your music: a kind of compromise that is extremely profitable, yet highly artificial at its core. You should write in your book that the theory you were taught only represents a later development in the history of our music – as long ago we used another "temporal tuning" system which our restitutive musicians, my son included, try to revive these days. Unfortunately I am bound by the promise I made not to introduce you too soon into the chronology of our music, yet I wouldn't want you to believe that everything started with the temporal equivalent of your Well Tempered Clavier.

The lack of trees made the dirt road retain more pluvial water, and, after a few hundred yards, the rut our gig's wheels were following started to go astray. As a matter of consequence, surprised by the physical effort we were now forced to make, Jean-Philippe went silent, unharnessed himself and turned on the mechanism whose spring we had constantly and unnoticeably wound up during the night. Now we were not feeling like a couple of haulers anymore, but rather like a pair of helmsmen. I was still intrigued by the feeling that, in spite of a sleepless night, I now thought of sleeping as an ignoble disease that I wasn't able to cure in due time.

The cultivated land, Jean-Philippe told me, generally heralds the proximity of the big cities. In their world, the latter are a combination of university campus, a residential area and a commercial hub. No big industry, though, because that is simply non-existent. Who knows, maybe one day, after the music theory book I am supposed to write will have been published, I will find time to describe the social fabric of the Temporalist world, as it is now shaped by the Brain Revolution: a utopia that seems impossible to graft over our digital era.

Jean-Philippe became more and more plaintive and started making pathetic statements about feeling French again in my company, and about the burden of teaching me Temporal Harmony in the way agreed upon by those who planned my mental trip to their world. He pestered me with disparate phrases that I could not make much sense of, as I had no idea what the theory I would have to learn would be about. The things I am about to find out in the following weeks or months, Jean-Philippe says, will equate the musical mindset of a European child who thinks that music is something between a four-voice choral harmony and Carl Czerny. I can read in his eyes the pathetic despair of those East-European intellectuals who, in the early 90s, would come to Paris to show us how well-informed, cultivated and "deep" they were, and how they would conquer us using "the true French culture" that in the past fifty years we only managed to destroy. Jean-Philippe's gesticulation became that of a swerving horse. He perspired heavily under the scorching sun, but at least he was constantly drinking water from the flask.

J.-P.: You will learn the Temporal Harmony that, *mutatis mutandis*, one would need to harmonize stupid little ditties. You will spend the last period of your stay here listening to records of our music from all periods, and learning how to follow it on the score. That will help you judge our theory within the frame of a certain kind of creativity that is imbued with historical contexts and stylistic justification.

I got thirsty too, so I asked Jean-Philippe to hand me over the flask. I took two sips from it and all of a sudden I understood the other mule's effusions: the receptacle contained the "Korean plum wine" that I had time to get friendly with in the preceding days.

I have rapidly read the pages I wrote so far and I am appalled by the fact that they look like the first chapters of a novel. I should speed things up and place us in Doktor Schmütz's etc. chalet – the place where I was taught the theoretical system which I am going to outline in this book.

Herr Doktor's chalet easily sticks out in its urban environment as the only building situated outside the various Temporalist architectural styles. The professor had indulged in the eccentricity of having copied the Bavarian house belonging to one of the German scholars whose body he had once worn. That happened back in the '60s, when he was very much interested in the research facilities available at the Max Planck Gesellschaft. As for the interior, I was surprised to notice that in great admiration of the Teutonic spirit he had it decorated with *fleur-de-lis* motifs. A young woman, who seemed to be both his personal assistant and Clara Morgane's twin sister, invited us into a living room that was illuminated through a multicolored Gothic Glaswand decorated with miniature stained glass scenes. The other end of the room was dominated by a massive fireplace. I was intrigued to see that the old psychologist owned a five octave rückpositiv with a single sheet on its stand: The hand copy of a well known Bach Choral. *(August, 2008. I have just found out its name:* Ach, was soll ich sünder machen?*)*

Jean-Philippe translated "Clara's" words for me: we shall soon be served lunch and then be given accommodations in two separate rooms. In the evening, when the professor has finished his academic duties, we shall start our lessons. I discreetly ask my guide whether the young lady is Herr Professor's daughter or niece – only to find out that, unlike musicians, psychologists "enjoy certain privileges".

Now I can clearly see why so many Temporalists dream of becoming psychologists. For no apparent reason, Jean-Philippe explained to me how frustrating it is to be incarcerated for two whole years in the body of some "retired" senior citizens or of some venerable old ladies, especially in Paris and particularly when in real life you are a man in your prime years. For instance, Monique anticipates how sore she will get each time her husband travels for a few minutes (indeed, two years for him) to Paris.

How I wish I had a cup of hot tota tea on my desk! It's been almost eleven hours since I started to write and cross out paragraphs and pages and, for the first time in the past two years, I feel that drowsy state that usually precedes sleep engulfing my mind, like a once familiar place that you have not visited in many years. I am unable to remember the taste of coffee! The cup that I emptied this morning is still on the desk... Hmm, the last drop is like Proust's madeleine: I have to rest content with this particular "old friend", so that tomorrow I finally introduce the main topic of this book.

– You-music! That's all that you will do in Europe with our great tradition! You-music!

Professor Schnitzel etc. is the embodiment of *der zerstreute Professor* and the only spectacled Temporalist I ever met in the two long years that followed. With one big difference, though: he is wearing the glasses in order *not* to see what happens around him. His eyes are closed most of the time, or perhaps open inwards, toward the revolution of his own brain. Any eyelid movement is harshly punished by the aching mist of the two magnifiers that make the glass lenses. Usually, that happens whenever the old psychologist gets angry and, tormented by the usual ocular pain, he utters one of his favorite words, "Scheisse!" and "Bollocks!". As all Temporalists naturally have that state-of-wonder facial expression that I first took notice of in the concert hall, the fact that the goggled eyes of our professor looked like a pair of turtle eggs made him an excellent candidate for a "Who will illustrate bewilderment for the new edition of the Temporalist Encyclopedia?" contest. For the reasons mentioned, I would rarely come across that particular entry.

(Summer of 2008)

I have finally found out what "you-music" means. It is not an English word (that is why I was unable to find it in my unabridged Webster), but a German expression – U-Musik – a shortened version of Unterhaltungsmusik, *meaning "light music", probably pop. From the same source I found out that the more elevated music is situated at a three-vowel distance:* E-Musik.

Herr Doktor summoned Jean-Philippe to an unknown direction and asked me to be patient. I would find out only lately that in the following hour my musical guide had been subject to a "cortical and sub-cortical optimization" process that enabled him to represent instantly, yet approximately, what Herr Schmelzinger etc. would say in English – a cognitive capacity very much simplified by the many Romance words imported into this Germanic language. In a few months I would experience myself a similar optimization of the brain that became extremely useful for my understanding of what students, researchers or professors from the Temporalist schools and universities that I have visited had to tell me. One cannot imagine the uncanny feeling of not understanding things that you clearly represent. At first I would be told a word in their language and, in that language still, Jean-Philippe would ask me what that word meant. My answer, in French, would be something like "I have no idea what «bird» means". "Bird?", my guide would repeat the French word that I had just uttered. "Oh, yes, bird!" I would then exclaim, not knowing what to make of that strange situation. Other times I would say that I didn't understand a jot, yet Jean-Philippe would ask me to draw the noun I had just "heard". I would then draw on paper the outlines of a coffee cup, upon which my guide would ask me what that looked like. "It doesn't look like anything!" I would reply. "A coffee cup?" he would insist. "What do you know…" would come my final reply while I would look over the recently drawn lines, seeing that they could hardly represent anything but a cup. These daily exercises helped me gradually link these representations to what Herr Professor called "the André Pogoriloffsky idiolect".

(Summer of 2008)

After reading the previous paragraph, my wife (who is convinced that I suffer from the inferiority complex of a failed musician – and that's why I wrote this book) tells me that she saw something similar in a TV documentary: a man with a brain condition was presented a written word like "telephone" that he would look at with one eye, upon which he would say that he has no idea what that word meant, yet that he would be able to draw it on paper. He would do just that and then say that he was unable to name the object he had just drawn.

33

I tell my wife that I clearly cannot invent such things. She replies that the only moment she was inclined to believe that my Temporalist journey was real happened while reading about the sexual appetite of the returning men after one of those two year long trips.

I think that the chronological depiction of my Temporalist adventure has now reached a deadlock, since I assimilated the theoretical principles of Temporalist music, in unequal portions, over the following two years. I will outline them here, trying to be as faithful to my memory as I possibly can, and adding things that I learnt from other musicians that I met after the few initiatory weeks spent in the Bavarian chalet.

There is no equivalent in Temporalist music theory for the European concept of tempo. There are no beats (regular underlying pulse), bars, time value augmentation or diminution (at least not in the way we currently understand them). There are no proper words for terms such as half, quarter, eighth or sixteenth notes, etc.

The only thing resembling, to the slightest degree, the idea of "tempo" is the 50 millisecond (50 ms) temporal grid. The first consequence of this convention is that all musical durations are multiples of this value: 100 ms, 150 ms, 200 ms etc.

It is interesting to note that, although most Temporalist musicians only know of these durational multiples, they cannot perform isochronous rows of 50 ms pulsations, as that is usually beyond their technical ability. Even "full throttle" virtuosi who can temporarily reach this speed cannot sustain it accurately for an indefinite period of time. I was told that the 50 ms pulse is perceived rather like a crackling than like a proper tempo. Dr. Sch... etc. informed me that in European terminology this sensation is called *crepitus* and that we know it quite well if we remember what a mechanical clock alarm sounds like.

Jean-Philippe tells me that the Temporalist word for this temporal grid has no exact correspondent in the French language, but it is quite close to terms such as "definition" or "resolution". To Temporalist music, the 50 ms resolution is something similar to the 72 pixels per inch standard used in Internet digital photography. Optionally, children learn to discriminate this resolution in the second grade, when they are presented several crepitus isochronous rows of pulsations and subsequently asked to tell the "musical" one. I do not recollect the other values presented (40ms, 60ms?), but I distinctly remember that the cracklings differed sufficiently for me to be able to distinguish them. It is interesting that all the children subjected in my presence to this test were able to tell the 50 ms isochrony. And yet, this test is not at all important in their curriculum. As I said, real music only makes use of the 50 ms multiples and only these are recognized by Temporalist musicians, and those with an absolute temporal hearing are able to produce them with great accuracy. Jean-Philippe repeatedly made a comparison with the European musicians that benefit from natural perfect pitch perception. The approximately 3% of humans who enjoy this genetic and cognitive gift won't be disturbed at all if the "oboe's A", that they instantly recognize, has a 441 HZ or 439 Hz frequency, instead of 440 Hz precisely. *Mutatis mutandis*, the same thing is valid in the Temporalist musical system: 50 ms is obviously not a value set in stone, as it permanently allows for small positive or negative deviations, most times compensatory – and that seems natural since musical durations in general are not produced by some infallible mechanics, but by human beings. Larger deviations from the 50 ms grid are immediately noticed by Temporalist musicians as "false durations" that have to be corrected. Jean-Philippe tells me that the 50 ms standard may be compared to our violinists' ability to play tempered music on their non-tempered instruments and to recognize and adjust false notes. A Temporalist concert that starts and continues with false durations, I was told, is a guaranteed fiasco. As in their world there are no conductors, only the equivalent of our concertmasters, it is customary that an experienced musician offer at the beginning of a performance their "oboe's A", which in their case is the 200 ms isochronous pulsation.

I am glad to see that I finally managed to write the first pages dedicated to Temporalist music theory. I imagine that Jean-Philippe would be very proud of me. As I was actually warned, terminology has already become a hindrance. For instance, if you tell a Temporalist musician something about "the 200 ms pulsation", he or she will have to ponder your words for a while before realizing what you are getting at. In their tradition, each category of isochronous pulsations (e.g. 100 ms, 250 ms etc.) has a name, the same way our culture has names for the seven diatonic modes (e.g. Mixolydian, Dorian etc.). Professor Schönemüllerin etc. says that, if Europeans so wish, they are free to name all the isochronous temporal modes what they please. He also asked me to use an English acronym, IOI (inter-onset-interval) to define them. For instance, the 200 ms isochrony will be called from now on "IOI 200 ms".

Before the grid was invented, music theory was just one of the many marvelous inexact sciences that would lately trigger, as a backlash, the Brain Revolution. Temporal modes were initially known by their distinct ethos, and not by being related to any kind of grid. For instance, even the IOI 200 ms mode was performed four centuries ago rather as IOI 180 ms, just because in this shape it preserves its whole expressiveness. Larger modes, such as IOI 400 and beyond, were performed in a kind of well-harnessed *rubato*. I know of all these historical details from the many discussions Jean-Philippe and I had about his son and his career as a restitutive Temporalist musician. He and his fellow instrumentalists are of the opinion that pulsatory temperance only massacred the real musical culture of their civilization. Yet, I think this historical development opened, at the same time, the pathway for a series of complexities, very similar to those triggered by Bach's tempered tuning system.

As for IOI 200 ms, music students learn to relate all the other temporal modes to it before achieving the ability to relate any mode to any other mode or to itself. I will develop this subject in another section of this book.

It is widely believed that the first Temporalist musicians have discovered empirically that different rows of equal pulsations evoke different affects. The fact that back then there was no superimposition of voices meant arithmetical relationships (which are so important in our musical tradition) between the actual durations of pulsations, belonging to different temporal modes, were of no particular importance. A temporal mode was valid as long as it evoked the intended affect. I suppose that this blatant indifference toward inter-durational proportions (e.g. 1:2, 2:4, 1:3 etc.) might have been the result of the prevalently pulsatory nature of Temporalist language. "And because we don't have F-Musik!", Herr Schtrapp etc. insisted to add.

Thus, the first known composers inherited an oral tradition that was deeply rooted into the ears and perception of their audiences, and that was based on a series of temporal modes previously used for monodies – therefore displaying a quite exotic range of IOIs: ca. 120 ms, 180 ms, 250 ms, 400 ms. After the universal implementation of the 50 ms grid, to these initial modes others were added, and all were intensely "verticalized", superimposed in various ways, during the first great stylistic epochs of Temporalist music. It was then that the first multiple "pulsatory passages" – combinations of durations taken from different temporal modes – were invented and added to a swiftly changing tradition. In our music, apart from the dotted rhythms or swing, having two different time values, there are no such traditionally established pulsatory structures, containing more than two different note durations. One exception seems to be the Siciliana rhythm that Mozart so memorably used in some of his compositions:

When Jean-Philippe helped me explain to another musicologist what this rhythm meant in our culture, the poor Temporalist looked quite bewildered when I told him that we notate the proportions established between different note values (3:1:2, in this particular case) without communicating their actual duration. Then I made the mistake of telling him that in order to respect the character of the Siciliana, these three repeated durations should evoke "a pastoral atmosphere" – upon which the musicologist composed a face of bewilderment and remained silent, listening one more time to Jean-Philippe's translation. Then, after a few suspended moments, he asked, Jean-Philippe translated and I represented mentally the elements of the following question: "So… therefore the durations should be similar to those produced by some domestic animals who communicate over an uncultivated strip of land?"

It is probable that European music history would have followed a similar evolution, had we not adopted some vague tempo markings such as *largo, andante, allegro* or *presto* etc., and if the very idea of tempo referred to some isochronous rows of pulsations rather than to a complex of durations made of the beat plus its augmentations and diminutions.

Up until the years that followed the Brain Revolution it was widely believed that the reason why temporal modes are associated to distinct affects was of a purely cultural nature – the same way people educated within the Western musical tradition associate major chords with gaiety and minor chords with sadness. The gradual disclosure of human brain secrets would later baffle musicians, who thus found out that almost every temporal mode corresponds to a distinct psychophysical phenomenology, marked by a series of perceptual thresholds that I am about to describe in the following pages.

The fastest temporal mode professional musicians are able to rely upon for note-to-note synchronization is IOI 100 ms. Before the introduction of the 50 ms standardization, interpreters used a slower version of this mode, corresponding to ca. IOI 120 ms. Today, this obsolete mode survives in primary musical education because some of the young instrumentalists are yet unable to produce accurately ten equal pulsations per second. During the school holidays, they are often asked by relatives and neighbors whether they managed to master "the fast temporal mode" – the achievement of this particular skill being considered by laymen the threshold that separates amateurs from professional musicians. A completely nonsensical assumption, in my opinion.

However, IOI 100 ms is perhaps the only temporal mode that may pose some purely technical (or physiological) problems to professional instrumentalists. I said "may pose" because in the last few years their contemporary music witnessed the introduction of a series of derivative modes that partially circumvent the 50 ms temporal resolution, which are nothing but a few of the diminutions that we call "tuplets". Yet, before this later development, the old virtuosi realized that they were able to produce note-to-note synchronizations in a faster than IOI 100 ms mode, namely ca. IOI 83 ms. The synchronization can only be achieved if the pulsations are organized in groups of three notes, with the duration of the whole group being affixed to the 50 ms grid: ca. 83 x 3 = 250 ms.

Music theory books mention this temporal mode as the absolute limit for note-to-note synchronization. Yet, during the many months that I spent listening and following the scores of thousands of hours of Temporalist music, I found several solo passages (no synchrony, that is) that made use of another, even faster, derivative mode: IOI 66 ms (ca. 66 x 3 = 200 ms).

Professor Schneiderzeit etc. asked me to remember that, in our academic world, IOI 100-120 is known as the "subjective rhythmization threshold". The old professor said that whenever we listen to equally spaced, timbrally identical pulsations produced by a metronome, our brain tends to group its clicks in groups of two – tick-tack or tack-tick – that is, imposing on our perception either the metacrusical (accent–non-accent / thesis–arsis / TH–AR) or the anacrusical (non-accent–accent / arsis–thesis / AR–TH) rhythmical model. This rhythmization is produced independently of our will, by means of a top-down type of perception imposed by our brain over a physical reality that does not contain it. An illusion. This phenomenon disappears when the isochronous pulsations are considerably faster than ca. IOI 100-120 ms. That also explains the crepitus sensation that becomes fully perceivable at around IOI 50 ms. Yet, for the temporal mode presented in this chapter, the subjective hierarchization of pulsations in thesis (TH) and arsis (AR) values is fully present.

The Doktor told me that the reason why the IOI 100-120 ms temporal mode has such a pregnant character stems from the fact that it is placed on the threshold that marks the transition from the crepitus sensation to the first modes where subjective rhythmization becomes present. After two years of continuous contact with Temporalist music, I was able to recognize this temporal mode myself. Now it became to me as familiar as a major third, although I have noticed that I am still unable to sustain it accurately in any musical context, the way Temporalist performers are.

It is no wonder that the transposition of the temporal mode here discussed, from IOI 120 ms to IOI 100 ms, took place during a historical period when virtuosity and technical brilliance eclipsed for a while the speculative compositional spirit that had characterized the preceding stylistic period. IOI 100 ms is what Temporalist manuals define as "an artificial mode" that was convened upon for the sake of the 50 ms standardization. The 20 ms translation resembles the history of the seventh natural harmonic (or the sixth overtone) that, as a minor seventh interval, is placed within the tempered dodecaphonic system a few commas above its natural place. "A false note", that is, if we consider the spectral provenance of the diatonic scale, yet a perfectly tuned one within our current twelve-note system.

Temporal modes placed in between the *crepitus* sensation threshold (ca. IOI 50 ms) and the subjective rhythmization threshold (ca. IOI 120 ms) take over characteristics from both thresholds. IOI 50 ms does not trigger, at a perceptual level, TH-AR hierarchizations. An ascending or descending musical scale, performed in the IOI 50 ms (theoretical) mode will be perceived as a row of non-accents. If the scale is given a zigzagged profile, the pulsations marking the descending or ascending melodic climaxes will be subjectively perceived as accents.

These are accents that only appear within the context of temporal modes situated below the subjective rhythmization threshold. In Temporalist music theory, they are called directional accents. In the case of IOI 100 ms, this kind of accent perception, while residual, is not completely absent. We can still talk about directional accents. In real music, performed within the 50 ms grid system, IOI 100 ms passages composed for Temporalist virtuosi often times display combinations of rhythmical (i.e. prosodical) and directional accents that do not always coincide. The sensation triggered by this accentuation interplay is associated with interpretative brilliance. In the original mode, IOI 120 ms, this brilliance is sensibly diminished.

During the long years that witnessed the transition from the historical temporal modes to the 50 ms standard, IOI 120 ms and IOI 100 ms cohabited. Back then, composers using IOI 100 ms were not speculating the prosodical versus directional accentuation interplay that this temporal mode implicitly offers. Their compositions make use of the IOI 100 ms mode either in unidirectional passages or in pulsatory structures where directional and prosodical accents always coincide.

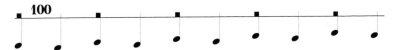

The fact that the 50 ms grid imposes the use of a series of artificial temporal modes, such as IOI 100 ms, makes this resolution create in Temporalist concert halls a peculiar atmosphere of musical familiarity, the same way we feel familiar with compositions created within the dodecaphonic tempered system, even though it contains a series of adjusted natural intervals, such as the tempered major third itself.

Both Jean-Philippe and Herr Professor advised me to totally ignore in this book the sonorous dimension of Temporalist music, just because "there is nothing to learn from it". The truth is that in their academic curriculum there are neither Harmony classes, nor professors to teach anything that would make music look like what we are used to call "the art of sounds". There is a telling parallelism between this state of facts and the reality that in our own big centres for music education there are no rhythm classes or departments, as there are no professors to teach exclusively musical time theory or at least the bar-rhythmical system. I found out from the old psychologist that in our Western hemisphere there actually are a few universities where musical time is given an important array of systematic studies. Yet these are mostly placed at the crossroads between music and cognitive psychology, while those implied in this recent development are either psychologists or musicians with a marked propensity towards the brain sciences. *Mutatis mutandis*, that is also the case in the Temporalist academic world: tonal harmony is a topic of narrow interest for their psychologists and an exotic discipline for musicians, Jean-Philippe being, as such, an exception.

If I were to find a concise formula, I would say that, in Temporalist music performance, the best chosen sounds are those that fully serve the sense and functionality of the temporal fabric belonging to a particular musical composition. There are a few basic rules acting rather like conventions, established by an unwritten interpretative tradition. Here are a few examples:

• in an AR-TH or TH-AR relationship, the AR pulsation will be interpreted as a lower note:

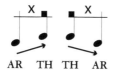

Temporalist composers never notate pitches, but only melodic trajectories. If the latter are not present in the score, interpretative conventions apply by default.

• generally, for temporal modes situated within the IOI 100-700 ms range, the faster the pulsations, the shorter the pitch intervals. The differences between "short", "medium" and "large" considerably varies from one musical instrument to another. For this reason, instrumental sections rarely play in unison, most times creating either a kind of heterophony or resembling the four-five note packages that usually perform the same rhythmical profile in the typical big-band arrangements.

• for orchestral compositions, the basic principle is that temporal layers, the superposing "voices", must be easily discerned by the listeners. That is why they will never occupy the same register. Temporalist composers notate in the score the precise display of these registers.

(Saturday, April the 12th, 2008)

After more than two years, I experienced again a couple of things that had previously seemed lost into a distant past: I made love to my wife and I SLEPT!

Here I am again in front of this blue notebook. However, last night I have only dreamt of writing music theory and now I have grasped the fine liner with the eagerness I used to have in the seventies and the eighties whenever I would extract the first Gauloises Caporal cigarette from the pack. I believe that yesterday I put on paper more words than I managed to write during the past two years as a whole. I wonder what kind of "optimization" my brain was subjected to, since I feel an unquenchable will to fill in page after page with my jagged and uneven writing.

To put an end to this chapter, I believe too that my guides were right in telling me that we have not much to learn from the way Temporalists relate their music to sounds.

The two years I spent there were divided into two periods: at first, Jean-Philippe and the Professor taught me the basic elements of general theory and temporal Harmony, while during the much longer second period I visited a great number of music schools and universities. There I would participate in some lessons, attend a concert or a conference – but most times I could be found in one of the audition rooms of the grand Temporalist music libraries where I would listen to records while following the music in the corresponding scores, imbuing my brain with the strains of Temporalist music written during the last four or five centuries.

By then I was already accustomed to ignoring apparent melodic lines and harmonic coincidences and focusing on the temporal plot of this or that musical composition. It is possible that my perception suffered that sudden accommodation Jean-Philippe told me about when he referred to those stereovisual illustrations. The Professor corrected our terminology telling us that the right word is not "accommodation", but "the AHA! moment". Thus, before my personal "AHA! moment", my purely subjective impressions regarding the sounds I would listen to while following Temporalist music evolved approximately this way:

A – a kind of Western contemporary music made of some cacophonous textures;

B – some microtonal textures;

C – some sonorous textures that seem to be governed by a logical set of rules;

D – a strictly necessary background – since discrete musical time cannot be perceived in the absence of a physical dimension to materialize it.

Professor Schwabenwein etc. allotted no less than two whole days to make me fully grasp the perceptual phenomenology concentrated in the area of the IOI 180-200 ms temporal mode. To Temporalists, this mode is laden with historical connotations as, contextually, both its versions were used: IOI 180 ms and IOI 200 ms, the latter once with the introduction of the 50 ms temporal resolution. Jean-Philippe suggested that I could make an association between this duality and the coexistence in European music of both the melodic minor mode and the harmonic minor mode. Those who understand the subtle difference between these versions would agree with Jean-Philippe's son when he states that "the 50 ms resolution spoiled for Temporalist music the chance of claiming itself, without any revolutionary turmoil, from its own tradition".

Before outlining the theoretical differences that set asunder the two faces of this temporal mode, I have to confess that my poor perception cannot tell them apart unless IOI 180 ms and IOI 200 ms are either superposed or placed in a fragmentary and alternative way, one after the other. My two guides told me that my incapacity to discern them is natural for a person who was brought up outside Temporalist musical practice. Had the time permitted and had I been encouraged to apply myself the things I have learnt – on the keyboard of the rückpositiv, for instance – the two instances of this mode would have became more apparent even to my untrained ears.

The weirdness of this mode probably stems from the fact that on its threshold two complementary perceptual phenomena meet or are in close proximity: one was placed by psychologists around the 180 ms value, while the other at around 200-220 ms.

The keyword for the first phenomenon is "mind-changing". It seems that the moment our brain gives an order to our fingers to press a note on a piano key, this order cannot be revoked during the first 180-200 milliseconds following its initiation. The musical implication of this psychophysical phenomenon is that any group of notes that circumscribe their attacks within this time-interval will contain one TH value only and will be the materialization of a single motor command. Doktor Schauspielerin etc. told me that in our academic world these motor commands along with their execution are called "actons", while actons situated within the 180-200 ms range are called "minimal actons". Unfortunately I am unable to recollect the details of his demonstration in which he stated that the 180-200 ms threshold is also important outside the discrete time framework (specific to music), namely for the continuous time perception, observed in the visual mode. I only remember that this interval is somehow linked to the threshold whence we say about an object that moves extremely slow that "it moves rather than stands still".

Of course, hundreds of years ago, the musicians who discovered and adopted the IOI 180 ms temporal mode had no idea what "actons" or "mind-changing threshold" mean. They simply noticed that the mode displays a peculiar expressiveness that may become familiar and thus returned to it whenever they felt it suited the utterance of certain emotional states.

During a later conversation with Jean-Philippe, I asked him how he explained, music theory notwithstanding, Temporalist sensibility around the distinct expressiveness of some temporal modes – some of which being in such close proximity that they are virtually impossible for an untrained ear like mine to discern. His answer seemed to me quite illustrative and commonsensical:

J.-P.: Temporal modes differ in a way that is similar to timbral discrimination. A B-flat produced by a violin, a clarinet, a French horn or a marimba will have the same frequency, yet people who acknowledge the variety of musical instruments will instantly recognize each specific timbre. The specificity of each timbre is given by the sound's envelope, amplitude and by the comparable intensity of the pitches that compose the harmonic spectrum of the fundamental note – B-flat in our case. Similarly, each temporal mode imaginable – that is, not only those pinpointed by tradition or by the 50 ms grid – is characterized by the presence of a combination of perceptual phenomena of which, from case to case, some just start to materialize, while others peak, while still others become residual.

Recognizing and mastering the temporal modes is an ability that is achieved in time, after a dedicated effort – but it is also a talent. Among Temporalists there are both people who are unable to discern two relatively distanced temporal modes and 3- or 4-year-old *wunderkinder* who can spontaneously tell the difference between, say, the IOI 180 ms and the IOI 200 ms versions of the temporal mode discussed in this chapter.

The keywords for the second phenomenon are "attention" and "perceptual present". In both musical worlds, average people, whose cognitive mechanisms are not altered in any way, perceive "the present moment" neither as an unquantifiable, abstract point in time (i.e. without a specific duration), nor as a temporal segment of a constant and precise length. "Experiential present", as Doktor Schöppel etc. called it, may have varying durations, yet its minimum span may be found around the 200 ms value.

Psychologists who studied the rate at which our brain moves from one object of consciousness to the next have observed that when subjects were asked to transfer as quickly as they can their attention from one object to another, the fastest such transfers took place after a 200-220 ms interval. The same sort of experiments established that this attention shift rate is not sustainable, that is, whereas changing one's attention from the second object to the third can still last about 200 ms, the uninterrupted attention shift from the third object to the fourth will always last more than ca. 200-220 ms. For all these reasons, the IOI 200 ms temporal mode is associated with "the maximum unsustainable rate of attention shift".

IOI 200 ms mode is also the first isochronous tempo that beginners can easily produce in a note-to-note synchronization. Professor Schneider etc. told me that in our system of temporal representation, based on the idea of musical beat, the ca. 200 ms interval represents the extreme threshold whence we can talk about this concept, that is so deeply rooted in our tradition.

The Brain Revolution has uncovered an interesting detail regarding the IOI 200 ms temporal mode. It was found out that, inexplicably, whenever young female instrumentalists get it wrong, they do that by attacking it in the IOI 180 ms version, whereas young male performers tend to slacken it down, performing it at around IOI 220 ms. With age, these sporadic deviations tend to disappear. The experimental discovery of this phenomenon was sufficient for the implementation of a relatively recent tradition: the oldest instrumentalist in an orchestra is always the one to give the Temporalist "oboe's A" – none other than the temporal mode described in this chapter.

During the first months of my Temporalist journey, I was quite intrigued by one particular thing: since one of their musicians can recognize instantly, say, the IOI 400 ms temporal mode, why on Earth does he or she not get to – by simple rhythmical deduction – the IOI 200 ms or IOI 100 ms mode? Why didn't I hear from my guides' lips, at least once, that IOI 300 ms is the augmentation of the IOI 150 ms temporal mode? The whole Western rhythmical system is based on such durational proportions. To my qualms, Jean-Philippe gave a simple yet bewildering answer: all Temporalist musicians are aware of these proportions which, in their culture, are simply musically irrelevant.

J.-P.: Which are the musical implications of the fact that a tritone is the double of a minor third? The latter is considered to be a consonant interval, while the tritone is viewed as a dissonance that even you don't construe mentally as the sum of two minor thirds or three whole tones, even though its name would say differently. Or indeed, which are the direct harmonic implications of the relationship between two chords such as C-E-G and C-G#-D? None, but I assure you that the latter's notes are twice as distanced in comparison to the major chord.

The word "assimilation" is a recurring commonplace in Temporalist musical education (Herr Professor advised me to use instead the term "absolute memorization"). There is a real obsession for the recognition and production of the temporal modes in spite of all conceivable jamming conditions. I was told about students asked to improvise scales in the IOI 200 ms temporal mode over recordings featuring non-musical modes such as, say, IOI 177, IOI 231 and IOI 277 ms. To some examiners, if the student still allows him- or herself to be influenced, or entrained, by the inertia of these jamming modes, that means that he or she did not "assimilate" sufficiently the uniqueness of that particular mode. The eleven- or twelve-year-old boys I saw passing this kind of test were quite pitiable…

I remember that, two or three years after I had started to study the piano, and after having warmed my mother's heart with some noticeable progresses, I cherished the idea of becoming a composer. By that time I had already jotted down a lame Scherzo, and my mother consulted a former high school colleague who meanwhile had became an orchestra conductor and who said that, in order to embrace such a demanding career, her son should have an extremely developed musical ear. The only way to achieve that would be a series of intensive solfeggio lessons. "Thank God we live in France!", added the conductor, God knows why.

A short time after this episode, our home was visited by miss Denoël, author of a booklet called *Vocal Exercises for All Levels* and the owner of a huge shopping trolley, laden with musical scores and other ledgers.

– André, tell me please – who is your favorite composer?

– Bach… I whispered.

– Wonderful! Now pick up a nice melody that you have studied recently and sing it with your voice.

I remember that I chose the F sharp minor *Prelude* from the second book of the *Well Tempered Clavier*, and that I started to sing the high voice to the best of my vocal abilities. After a few bars, the *Mademoiselle* interrupted me bluntly:

– Fine, that will do… Now I will play on the piano, in the same tempo, the next *Prelude*, in G major, which luckily has the same time signature. And while doing that I will sing the melodic line of your *Prelude*, in its original tonality.

Retrospectively, her ability to detach herself – completely, it seems – from the tonal polarizations looks to me both impressive (from a sporting point of view) and meaningless. It is the half-sublimated version of the puppy who worked hard under its trainer's supervision and now deftly pedals the unicycle. Miss Denoël promised me that if I were to equate her performance, the pathway to the really difficult solfeggios would surely open up for me.

This first encounter with a typical (or was it?) French solfeggio lesson was also the last. During the following weeks, the *Mademoiselle* was repeatedly told over the phone that *petit* André is immobilized in bed, shaken by a feverish bout of flu that wouldn't recede.

If we accept that miss Denoël's exercises mean "the interiorization of the tempered dodecaphonic system", then I was wise to have remained a passionate amateur pianist. Jean-Philippe, who went through all stages of the Temporalist musical education, is of another opinion:

J.-P.: It is true that our basic temporal exercises are arid and tedious, but they constituted for centuries the fastest way to musically modify and optimize the human brain. Every newly formed synapse that enables us to perceive in spite of tonal attractions or pulsatory inertia adds one more micron to the borderline that separates the brain of a musician from that of a simple music lover. Both our musical traditions imply the expansion of our perceptual acuity, whether we talk about pitches or combined temporal modes. When I first listened to *Passio Matthaeum*, I was convinced that your Jean Sebastien had experienced a Brain Revolution of his own or that he was actually exported to Europe from a parallel world. After that first impression, I read a few biographies and found out how much this man worked so that the polyphonic capabilities of the twelve notes become for him a second nature. In the absence of this initial effort, our musical cultures would display a completely different landscape... Listen to the works of your computer music composers. I suppose they are often times surprised themselves by the sound of their compositions, and that is precisely because they are incapable of elogizing them mentally. I remember that, while I was studying your pitch systems, at some point I had to learn about the second Viennese School and I was thrilled to discover that the twelve old sounds were able to create a completely different compositional universe. Yet, I was so disgruntled to find out that the things I learned during the first couple of days were basically everything that I was supposed to know about the system that was meant to ensure, for a long period of time, "the supremacy of German music". In the early seventies, I met a group of serial composers and I asked them whether, while listening to a late composition by Stravinsky, they were able to hear and transcribe the actual series used at a certain point. "No way!", was their unanimous reply – and that is why I decided to discard for good this chapter of my studies and enjoy, as a simple music lover, the harmonic eeriness that the representatives of this musical trend were able to create.

Before the implementation of the 50 ms grid, this mode did not exist. It was introduced just because it fitted the newly-invented temporal resolution and because there was a 100 ms long "empty place" created after the replacement of the IOI 120 ms mode with IOI 100 ms and of the IOI 180 ms mode with IOI 200 ms. This empty place insured the transition to and from some important perceptual thresholds of whose psychophysical characteristics the new mode was sure to be influenced, even if in a residual or incipient fashion.

Jean-Philippe, who never ceased to amaze me with his associations between the two musical cultures, told me that the IOI 150 ms temporal mode is more likely the IOI 100 ms' "sharp" than the IOI 200 ms' "flat" – and that is so just because the perceptual phenomena associated with IOI 180 ms and IOI 200-220 ms are not to be found in the set of psychophysical determinants that can define the IOI 150 ms temporal mode. Some Temporalist theorists are of the opinion that, in fact, this mode is actually a far-fetched version of the old IOI 120 ms. The musical practice that followed the implementation of the 50 ms grid showed that, derived or not, this temporal mode has its own "voice", that is definitely different from that specific to IOI 100 ms – a voice that musicians learned in time to assimilate and value. Here are just a few characteristics of the IOI 150 ms temporal mode:

- note-to-note synchronization is, of course, easier than it was in the case of IOI 100 ms, yet not easy enough for beginners, who at first can only master the IOI 200 ms and larger modes.
- the minimal acton will cover only two pulsations of this mode, whereas in the IOI 100 ms temporal mode it could encompass two or three. Researchers unveiled the fact that whenever ternary groupings are made of the IOI 100 ms mode, all three pulsations will obey the conditionals of the minimal acton:

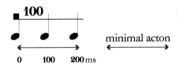

The fact that the third pulsation may be "mind-changed" in the IOI 150 ms mode seems to be essential for the human brain to discriminate between two temporal modes (i.e. IOI 100 and 150 ms) that are functionally so similar.

In a later discussion, Jean-Philippe told me that, during the years in which musicians were still debating the appropriateness of implementing such an artificial mode within the academic musical practice, a nineteen year old composer had the idea of writing a musical piece in which he speculated creatively upon the yet-to-be-discovered virtues of the IOI 150 ms isochrony. The result was a ten-minute-long Rondo (in our terms) for a string instrument. The composition soon became a hit and as such buried forever the hatchet of the previous debates.

J.-P.: This is why, as a musician, I cannot stand those scholars who are obsessed with being right. I am sure that today, ages after the outbreak of our Brain Revolution, if the same debate had appeared in our agora, some full-fledged psychologists would have solemnly decided that the IOI 150 ms mode may or may not become part of the theoretic inventory of our music. And they would be demiurgically right in either case. I admire your culture for many reasons, one of them being the fact that there is no tome titled "The Definitive Harmony Treatise of the French Academy". Unfortunately, in this world, every temporal innovation that is proposed by composers by means of their works is immediately dissected by a plethora of musicologists-converted-to-psychology who decide *Ubi et Orbi* whether our brain may or may not assimilate the respective temporal structures. A couple of centuries ago, uninspired pulsatory innovations were simply discredited by interpreters' indifference. This is why, dear André, I am a little bit scared that the description you will make of our musical tradition, as reformulated by Herr Professor, instead of reaching musicians, will get in the hands of some psycho-cognitive maniacs who will start to dissect every perceptual phenomenon that you will describe along with the corresponding temporal modes. Some will state categorically that this or that phenomenon is wrongly used, unsubstantiated or abusively speculated – and perhaps, punctually, they will be right. Let them bark, because one day a young musician who has read your book will pick up his or her violin or clarinet and, inspired by your effort, will discover that, indeed, musical time is much more than the bar-rhythmical system has to offer.

Despite the fact that, at some point, during the many months in which I and Jean-Philippe were gallivanting from one music school to another, pulling his gig around, one of the music teachers that I met did his best to describe to me the history of Temporalist music notations, the subject seemed too luxuriant for me to be able to memorize its chronology. I am truly unable to recall whether the syllabus-like notation preceded the dots-and-lines one, or if the latter went along with the proportional semiography. All that I know is that the standardised contemporary notation is still linked in some way to what Temporalists call "the natural flow of human speech" – an unfortunate abstraction that is unanimously accepted and that is associated with the way Temporalists imagine that an educated gentleman should speak. For all these reasons, the semiography I got so familiar with in the thousands of scores that I studied there does not stand a chance to be imported successfully into our world. From this point of view, both Jean-Philippe and Herr Schönschlager etc. were of the same opinion, but the reasons they had in mind when they suggested that I should not describe the contemporary notation in this book are of a historical nature...

Centuries ago, when Temporalist musicians started to consider for the first time the necessity of a music notation for their compositions, there were no metronomes (not that Temporalists ever had any) and no clocks able to measure milliseconds. What they had was a language whose words made sense by means of the duration of the interplay of its syllables and by means of the prosody thus formed. As a result, the few temporal modes that might have been used back then were associated with the length of certain syllables belonging to certain words – not the way John the fiddler mumbles them, but in the ludicrous manner of speech used by the educated apothecary who just opened his drugstore three blocks away. Things become even more intricate when we do not speak of single syllables, but of rows of three, having the same length. There are not too many words to contain such triplets, but I was assured that these are sufficient to cover, through association, all the known temporal modes, old and new, covering the whole IOI 100-400 ms range. As many of the early musicians who were supposed to read the first scores where illiterate, the mentioned words had to designate easily representable things such as "ladder", "leg" or "tree" etc. The corresponding object was then drawn on paper while above it a set of lines indicated the number of pulsations that the musician should play in that particular temporal mode. This is the way a whole history commenced...

The necessity for three isochronous syllables has a simple explanation: in order to avoid any possible confusion, a temporal mode should contain at least three pulsations. The first one opens up the mode, the second one establishes the duration while the third confirms it and, I was said, gives the final touch to the expressiveness of the respective mode.

Maybe later in this book I will find time to explain why Temporalists do not consider single durations or groups of two isochronous pulsations as real temporal modes. These are covered by a separate musical discipline that deals exclusively with the art of passing from one IOI to another.

Contemporary notation has long dropped those drawn objects and lines, but not the ridiculous association with the three syllables belonging to certain words – as they are currently uttered by the theoretical representatives of the most exclusivist academic community. Graphical symbols were invented for each and every duration that obeys the 50 ms grid (different symbols represent the old, traditional modes) – along with rules of graphical placement meant to indicate the direction of the melodic line. Other symbols delineate the prosodic contours. All these may be placed in a simple five-line staff, so that pulsations be associated to precise pitches but – I have to admit – that would make the actual music reading much too unwieldy. Doktor Schmalter etc. came in with a semiographic solution that is both simple and practical and that I have already used in the few examples scattered along the last paragraphs. Thus, pulsations are written just like our musical notes. It is just that the absence of the bar-rhythmical hierarchizations (that in our tradition predefine the placement of accents, secondary accents and non-accents) requires a separate symbolization of the thesis (TH) and arsis (AR) values:

TH   AR

The Professor insisted that the name of this musical notation be inspired from an English term – zeugma – originating from the Ancient Greek word *zeugnunai*, meaning "to yoke". I simply cannot ignore the will of the very inventor of this notation, and as such from now on, in this book, the examples will be written in the "zeuxilogic notation" while the pulsations (i.e. the actual musical notes) will be called "zeuximae". I asked permission from my guides to alternatively call this semiographic system "perceptual notation", just because its roots are to be found, indeed, within a series of temporal perception phenomena. The two Temporalists had nothing against my idea.

In order to visually discriminate between the various temporal modes, Professor Schakoschka etc. proposed that zeuximae be indicated the duration individually, if this imposes itself as a necessity…

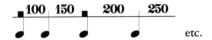

… and only as a kind of musical signature, whenever we operate with whole rows of zeuximae belonging to the same temporal mode:

J.-P.: The only problem with these figures is that people might think that the durations, expressed in milliseconds, are set in stone. We are not quartz watches and we shall never produce absolutely equal pulsations. The important thing is that pulsations seem equal for the educated perception of a musician who is already accustomed with the ways we understand musical time.

It was at that moment that Herr Schepp etc. felt obliged to provide me with a whole dissertation about the actual meaning of "durational evenness at the level of human perception". I am utterly unable to reproduce it entirely, but I will jot down the few things that I managed to remember.

For various IOIs, the deviations from the isochronous flow are detected differently by human perception. The English term that Herr Professor used was the "Just Noticeable Difference" (JND). This JND has either an absolute value (measurable in milliseconds) or a proportional value (measured in %), depending on the IOI that we want to consider. Both values were presented to me, but I am unable to recall the details of this scientific explanation. As long as the deviations from the isochronicity of a temporal mode are situated below the JND threshold, our brain is unable to detect them. If the deviations exceed the JND threshold, Temporalists consider that the instrumentalist indulged in an agogical license that may or may not be considered acceptable. Finally, if the JND threshold is exceeded in an exaggerated manner, Temporalists consider that the interpreter is simply out-of-time or temporally false. I found it interesting to learn that, even if we do not consciously perceive the positive or negative deviations situated below the JND threshold, our brain detects them subliminally and corrects them by means of a compensation process that makes the real durations produced by an interpreter look like a zigzag placed around the intended durational value:

As the absolute or proportional values of the imperceptible deviations vary from one temporal mode to another, they contribute to the distinct expressiveness of each and every IOI.

Just a few minutes ago I wrote that I was unable to remember the way the JND evolves from one temporal mode to another. Well, my still "optimized" brain perhaps received the distress signal, consulted its zillion neurons and suddenly projected on the screen of my consciousness Doktor Schimberg's etc. words: "Six milliseconds for IOIs faster than 240 ms and 2,5% for IOIs slower than 240 ms".

The IOI 250 ms temporal mode is the modern version of the old IOI 240 ms mode. Few Temporalist musicians are actually able to discern the two if they are not juxtaposed in some way. I find it incredible how the old musicians, who had no idea of the "just noticeable difference" concept, somehow felt that somewhere around IOI 240 ms "something" was taking place and chose to add the corresponding temporal mode to their musical inventory. Ironically, the "hieroglyph" illustrating this mode originally represented a fence stile.

The peculiarity of the IOI 250 ms mode stems from several perceptual incidences. For instance, there are certain pulsatory structures that cannot be turned back (i.e. "mind-changed"), although the attacks of the pulsations they are composed of fit within the 200-250 ms span – larger, therefore, than the 180-200 ms timespan, specific to the minimal acton. It seems that beyond the 250 ms threshold any pulsatory structures may be "mindchanged", these obeying no more the "undetourability" of the minimal acton (whose specific threshold remains within the 180-200 ms zone for any other pulsatory structure). My guides told me that because of these characteristics, the IOI 100, 150, 200 and 250 ms temporal modes group themselves into a kind of modal family, whereas temporal modes from the IOI 300-700 ms range create another one that I shall describe in due time. Professor Schmältzer etc. pointed out to me that my own predecessors made this distinction as well when they observed that the first equal pulsations that may be perceived as beats are situated around the MM = 208 (beats per minute) value, corresponding to a theoretical IOI 288 ms temporal mode...

After a lengthy ransacking of my closet, garage, attic, basement, balconies and pantry, I have finally found my old Wittner metronome and, indeed, the fastest beat the contraption is capable of reproducing is 208 beats per minute.

The common trait of the four temporal modes situated within the IOI 100-250 ms range is a certain "agogical unavailability". At some point Herr Schmilstein etc. invited me to sit on the rückpositiv bench and improvise isochronous melodies in the tempi suggested by

Jean-Philippe, none other than the four debated IOIs. I preferred not to improvise but, since I knew it by heart, to perform the D major *Prelude* from the first book of the Well Tempered Clavier:

I have just returned from the piano. I was unable to play it from memory although I know that I performed it repeatedly during the last week... it is just that "the last week" included a two year long intermission...

The moment I attacked the isochronous sixteenth notes of the *Prelude* in what I believed to be the IOI 100 ms temporal mode, the two guides were unable to hide, beyond thinly veiled encouraging smiles, their grimaces. It is probable that, to their ears, my interpretation was so false temporally that under other circumstances I would have been greeted with paper bags filled with mustard, thrown directly at my face.

– Now try to maintain... roughly this temporal mode and add to it a *quasi-rubato* interpretation by placing here and there little agogical accents, Jean-Philippe asked me.

I tried to do just that but I was unable to – or I was able to the extent doubling the duration of some of the sixteenth notes could be considered "agogical accentuation". The same phenomenon repeated in the case of IOI 150 ms and IOI 200 ms temporal modes, although the fact that these were slower should have allowed me to place some less exaggerated agogical accents. The Professor explained to me that there is an unseen conflict between my will to accentuate expressively some of the notes and the programming of the actons as groups of two or more pulsations. I was not more successful with the IOI 250 ms temporal mode, although I felt that it was more prone to expressive timing.

J.-P.: This is why even *your* musical literature has no oxymoronic indications such as *presto rubato*. The phenomenon you have just experienced – and the culprit for the agogical unavailability – is called pulsatory inertia. It is specific for temporal modes situated within the IOI 100-250 ms range and, as we shall see, it maintains an ever waning residual value in the case of temporal modes from the IOI 300-700 ms range.

Professor Schwimmer etc. added that, whenever the inertial modes are present for a longer period of time, they act as a kind of attractors for the perception of the instrumentalists who are supposed to perform other pulsatory structures. This is why it became so important in Temporalist musical practice that all temporal modes be solidly assimilated by instrumentalists, so that the attractors be not necessarily ignored, but "counterpointed" in a resolute manner. The phenomenon of losing the temporal grip due to the presence of such an attractor is known in the English terminology as "entrainment". The phenomenon does not manifest in the case of isochronous pulsations belonging to the *crepitus* category.

Although I have already mentioned the importance of assimilating the various modes in the Temporalist educational curriculum, I think I should write here a few words about the impression made upon me by a recent composition that I listened to during a concert. It was written for three temporal voices that almost permanently superimposed different inertial modes, each acting as an attractor for the other two. The author also used some of the old, traditional IOIs, so that the three instrumentalists had to perform in the same time temporal modes such as IOI 100, 120 and 180. The composition itself was not a masterpiece but I found it remarkable that the three virtuosi managed to look both creative and precise in the midst of such a premeditated jamming.

After having explained all these, my guides asked me to play again the D major *Prelude*, this time in a new temporal mode, suggested again by my dear Jean-Philippe. Now, indeed, the tempo felt aerated enough so that my agogical licences be able to alter expressively the linear pace of Bach's sixteenth notes. I was actually playing the most beloved temporal mode of the Temporalist "romantics": IOI 300 ms, the first in which we are able to allot one acton per pulsation – this very fact placing it amongst the IOIs characterized by "agogical availability". Professor Schaumbad etc. pointed out that my agogical accents *must* overcome the JND in order to be perceived as such. The sudden waning of the pulsatory inertia in IOI 300 ms offered my brain the necessary respite to make decisions regarding the expressive inequality of pulsations. He then quoted a few experiments conducted in my world, in which professional musicians were asked to categorize different IOIs either as "divisions of a musical beat", "divisions rather than actual beats", "beats rather than divisions" or "musical beats". The results of these experiments confirmed the fact that the border between continuity and discontinuity is to be found somewhere in between the IOI 250 ms and IOI 300 ms temporal modes. In this 50 ms long span, Herr Doktor, told me, our brain switches from a holistic interpretation of pulsations to a note-by-note one.

Between IOI 200 ms and IOI 400 ms, pulsations may be regarded consciously (through a top-down representation) both holistically and in a note-by-note manner (by an arbitrary transfer of attention from one pulsation to the next). We have seen that in the case of the IOI 200 ms mode, this transfer is not sustainable. It remains unsustainable for the IOI 250 ms and IOI 300 ms temporal modes, but our effort to voluntarily pass from one object of consciousness to the next (musical pulsation in our case) becomes less and less strenuous. The IOI 400 ms Temporalist musical mode is the first one in which, with a minimal effort, we are able to transfer our attention from one pulsation to the next in a sustainable manner. Psychophysicians of our world established that the complete transfer of attention takes place only starting with the IOI 600 ms mode, where there is no apparent effort required from us to move from one object of consciousness to the next, for an indefinite period of time. Jean-Philippe pointed out to me that all temporal modes in which the attention transfer involves a certain effort imply a peculiar phenomenon that musicians of our world have long discovered and consequently called it "secondary accentuation". Thus, in all temporal modes of the IOI 200-500 ms range, whenever we organize pulsations metacrusically, in groups of four, we may perceive the third note as an accent of a different temporal functionality (in comparison to the main accent, of the first pulsation).

It now becomes clear that I have to dedicate a separate chapter to the different types of accents that Temporalist musicians operate with. I also failed in my attempt to introduce the temporal modes in their natural order, as I initially planned to do. Yet, I could not avoid introducing the temporal modes families and the interaction of some perceptual phenomena with various categories of IOIs. I also hope that musicians who had the patience to read my book thus far are not getting confused by the multitude of new terms and concepts that I had to introduce in the previous pages. At least that is how I felt during the first days spent in the Bavarian house of mister Schloss etc., but I had the privilege of being assisted in my fuzziness by two equally courteous scholars.

Returning to the secondary accents, Temporalists consider that in four pulsation metacrusical groups belonging to the IOI 150 ms mode, the perception of the third note as a secondary accent is "residual". In fact, the TH versus AR value of the respective pulsation is still debated in their academic community.

J.-P.: If you will, this mysterious pulsation is similar to your minor-major or moll-dur chord, in which the third is placed in between the known minor and major thirds. In our case, it seems that the debate is not alien from the fact the IOI 150 ms mode was speculatively imposed by the implementation of the 50 ms grid. Before that, it used to be clear that in IOI 120 ms the third pulsation of the group is not a secondary accent while in IOI 180 ms – it is.

Thus, Temporalists consider that the third pulsation belonging to a metacrusical group of four, in the IOI 100 ms mode, is not perceived by us as a secondary accent. Anyway, in their tradition this kind of categorization (i.e. accent, secondary accent, non-accent) is far more complex than what our bar-rhythmical system was able to crystallize. I hope I will be able to remember and write down all the details regarding this interesting topic. Finally, all secondary accents not being usually meant as TH values by interpreters are notated as AR zeuximae.

I should start this chapter by saying that the ways AR pulsations may group around a TH value is not the subject of "the art of pulsatory groupings", a Temporalist musical discipline whose existence I have already mentioned in the previous pages. In the following paragraphs I shall only present the prosodical formulae, based on the TH-AR dichotomy, currently used in Temporalist music

Jean-Philippe suggested that, in describing the possible interpulsatory relationships, I should use two terms borrowed from the bar-rhythmical theory. Thus, between a TH pulsation and one or more AR pulsations there can exist *anacrusical* and *metacrusical* relationships. In the absence of the bar-rhythmical system, in which in most cases the TH and AR values are topologically predetermined, the two terms seem quite inadequate to me, if not simply improper. I would have rather used the term of "antecedence" for anacrusical relationships and "subsequence" for the metacrusical ones. Yet, I shall respect the suggestion of my musical guide as I was unable to find better terms in other languages. The German words *Auftakt* and *Abtakt* too conspicuously hint at the idea of musical beat, and so do the English terms *upbeat* and *downbeat*.

The prosodical formulae derived from the two kinds of interpulsatory relationships gain significance depending on the temporal mode on whose ground the actual pulsations interact. For instance, an anacrusical relationship in an inertial temporal mode is supplementarily "welded" by the holistic perception of the consecutive pulsations. On the other hand, in larger temporal modes (e.g. IOI 700 ms) an anacrusical relationship must be constructed mentally, through a conscious cognitive effort. Interpulsatory relationships become immensely more complex when we deal with the art of pulsatory groupings, the supreme discipline of Temporalist music, in which anacrusical, metacrusical and combined relationships often times imply pulsations belonging to different IOIs (and other temporal artifices that I shall hopefully find time to write about).

For all these reasons, in this chapter I shall only bring up the basic interpulsatory relationships and the ways in which these are notated within the semiographic system invented by Doktor Schagenspeer etc. Thus, anacrusical relationships will be symbolized by a slur always pointing *outside* the actual zeuximae:

  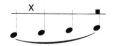

Metacrusical relationships will be symbolized by a slur pointing *towards* the actual zeuximae:

In Temporalist music, there also are anacrusical-metacrusical relationships:

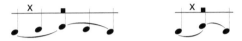

I am familiar with the AR-TH-AR anacrusical-metacrusical relationship from the d minor *Prelude* (the first book of the Well Tempered Clavier):

In principle, adjoining pulsations that do not establish an anacrusical or metacrusical relationship are considered to be in a relationship of prosodical indetermination. There are several types of such indeterminations. Here are just a few of them:

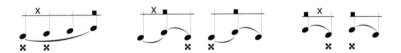

In the first example there is a prosodical indetermination relationship established between two AR pulsations belonging to the same pulsatory structure; in the second, the two AR values belong to different pulsatory structures while in the third example the indetermination is established between an AR and a TH pulsation.

In order for you to have a glimpse at how much things complexify in the art of pulsatory groupings, I shall give just one example:

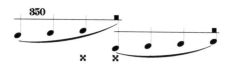

The first pulsatory structure in this example is an acton (N.B. – not a *minimal* acton!) made of an anacrusical relationship AR-AR-AR-TH. As the chosen temporal mode is sufficiently distanced from what we have previously defined as the threshold of mind-changing, when the interpreter attacks the first TH pulsation, he or she arbitrarily changes his or her mind and commences a new AR-AR-AR-TH anacrusical structure. Temporalist musical literature is a wealth of such artifices that constitute the gist of a musical universe which I could hardly believe we could have ever invented by ourselves.

Returning to the last example, the question is what kind of prosodical relationship is being established between the third AR and the fourth, the latter marking the outset of the second anacrusical structure. Is it a relationship of indetermination? A "thwarted" anacrusical relationship? If so, the fourth pulsation is a TH for the first structure and an anacrusical AR for the second?

Such ambiguities nurture in fact the lofty philosophy of Temporalist musical composition – as even after so many generations after the Brain Revolution, these musicians do not have answers for all the questions raised by the discrete-temporal competence of the human mind.

Herr Schmüller etc. told me that while he was "spying" the libraries and archives of the Max Planck Institute in Leipzig, München, Berlin and Nijmegen, he established an intellectual friendship with a Bavarian psychologist who, during his childhood and adolescence, had studied in depth, like myself, piano playing and the academic musical disciplines. He was of the opinion that valuable systems are valuable in themselves, even if people are unable to sublimate them in the masterpieces that would confirm their inherent value. German language, the Bavarian scholar claimed, would remain an ideal environment for philosophy even in the absence of the well known German thinkers and of their impressive body of work. The same way, Tonal Harmony used by *Schlagerkomponisten* remains *in nuce* a great system, even if in the case of U-Musik "it gets perverted by the infantile *teloi* of some musicians who only encourage their own mediocrity".

It seems that the Bavarian psychologist was a radical snob, but the idea that captured Doktor Schnittke's etc. attention followed these words as a logical follow-up.

The German scholar was of the opinion that the grandiose systems are those that are capable to host a certain type of creativity, optimally placed in the no-man's-land that separates total determination from total indetermination (chaos, that is). Thus, functional harmony couldn't possibly have materialized its own abstraction in such a convincing manner had the chordal relationships been immutable or, to the contrary, had people had reason to believe that any chord may follow (with equal consequences) any other chord.

Starting from this point, Herr Schopenhauer etc., who surely is what Germans call *ein philosophische Kopf*, delivered to me a whole lecture on "the ontic superiority" of Temporal Harmony in comparison to the sonorous, European, one. (It seems that one simply cannot enthusiastically embrace the undisputable values of the German culture without significantly altering the meaning of one specific word: "superior".) The Temporalist professor claimed that our Western civilization "wouldn't have made such a mockery", in the last decades, of its own musical tradition, had the ways the human brain relates to sounds secured survival, food, orientation in time and space or procreation. If the sonorous polarizations had such an existential fundament, Western musicians would have paid infinitely more care in infringing upon the laws that seem to constitute the Harmonic Code:

Herr Sch. etc.: You may design a building that defies the laws of gravity, but not one that breaks them, because you will only be the author of a big pile of *roubles!*

(Summer of 2008)
My wife, who is the real English speaker in our family, tells me that the professor had probably intended to say "rubble" and ineptly added an "s" at the end of the word. Well, a big pile of golden roubles is an equally interesting image…

The old psychologist hinted, of course, to our contemporary composers – a mere bunch of *Papiermusik* creators, in his opinion, with whose plenipotentiary representative he mistook me for no apparent reason. Every time Herr Schapst etc. heated up, Jean-Philippe would smile to me meaningfully, as if to say that I should let him get tired of his own tumultuousness. Whenever his indictments seemed to create a tedious loop, the door on the right side of the fireplace would burst open and mademoiselle Morgane would pace the room with a plate in her hands, providing the Professor with some gelatinous pills and a few mysterious words whispered in his hairy ears, that would make the venerable psychologist stand still, yet slightly impatient, like a good dog who is shown the soon-to-be-served meal.

After such a ritual, the professor continued his argument by saying that the laws of Temporal Harmony are not the consequence of an elective aesthetic, as they partake of the fundamental data of the way our species managed to adapt itself, in order to survive, to the discrete nature of time. Thus, Temporal Harmony benefits from an existential eco-logic that is based on the psychophysical mechanisms of attention, reaction capability, anticipative projections or, as we have seen, the power to turn back previous intentions etc. All these get harmonized into a set of rules that are most times immutable, in some cases re-formulatable by means of perception enhancement, and rarely of a purely aesthetic nature. That is what provides the Temporal Harmony Code with a certain stability.

The professor insisted that there is nothing similar from this point of view in "the grand system of functional Harmony" in which most of the rules, if not all, are of a purely aesthetic nature. An aberrant harmonic relationship does not "hurt" the way it hurts Temporalist instrumentalist when they try to perform some pulsatory formulae "the way these were imagined by some Temporalist composers whose only aim is to flummox the audience".

Here, Temporalist music theory considers that we deal with one single mode whose graphical symbol used to be, originally, some kind of pig. Its evident agogical availability resulted in its overuse by early musicians, "the pig's mode" thus becoming the first known non-isochronous tempo. Back then, interpreters used *ad libitum* durations lasting from (approximately) 280 ms to 370 ms per pulsation. For a European ear, this music, still cultivated by their ancient music nostalgics, may sound like the *rubato* performance of an uncertain tempo. In reality, musicians never come too close to the powerful perceptual thresholds situated at around IOI 250 ms and IOI 400 ms.

With the introduction of the 50 ms grid, the mode theoretically kept its agogical availability while being in fact "tempered" by the implementation of the two instances that are currently described in all Temporalist music theory schoolbooks: IOI 300 ms and IOI 350 ms.

By the time the two guides started describing to me "the pig's mode", everybody could feel a kind of thaw in our human interactions, especially in the overt hospitality of our hosts, Herr Professor and Clara. The lessons were often times interrupted by divagations, sheer chitchat, by psychologist's philosophical tempests and by meal breaks that were followed by short active siestas in which I was asked to improvise "anything" on the rückpositiv's keyboard. After each such extemporization in which I would vamp approximate melodies with my right hand, accompanied in the lower register by simple chords, Jean-Philippe would encourage me by asking the same silly question: "And all that you have improvised is coming exclusively from your brain?" That was the moment when the two Temporalists would exchange a few significant glances whose meaning was something like "you see it is true?".

It seems that musicians who were preponderantly exposed to the Western musical tradition, when asked to improvise something, spontaneously chose a tempo whose binary divisions are situated in the area of the temporal modes discussed in this very chapter – whereas in the Temporalist *Weltanschauung,* in which musicians have been exposed to a wholly different kind of musical tradition, only their few vocal interpreters chose to improvise spontaneously in the pig's mode area, while the instrumentalists prefer to display their artistry in faster temporal modes and by means of more intricate pulsatory structures that would better demonstrate their virtuosity.

Doktor Schütz etc. told me that he has no idea whether we prefer the circa 600-700 ms beat or its binary divisions (at around 300-350 ms).

Most time-psychologists whom he met during his Euro-American peregrinations were inclined to believe that it was the beat and not its division. One of the arguments in favor of this hypothesis was that around 600-700 ms the attention transfer from one beat to the next is not only sustainable, but also comfortable. Secondly, starting with the 600 ms beat, the possibilities for musical duration-splitting peak, as a 600 ms long crotchet may be divided rhythmically in no less than four ways, all corresponding to some of the temporal values that I have already commented upon in the previous chapters: IOI 100, 150, 200 and 300 ms.

It is because of the fact that IOI 300 ms and IOI 350 ms temporal modes are instances of the same kind of pulsatory functionality that their separated assimilation poses some degree of difficulty. A hindrance in this respect is their very agogical availability, as here the inertial character is much less poignant than in the case of the modes from the IOI 100-250 ms range. In Temporalist music schools, pupils who have already assimilated the IOI 150 ms mode use the simple trick of linking rhythmically and briefly two such short pulsations only to continue the IOI 300 ms mode as a standalone isochrony. For the IOI 350 ms mode they use a contraption that only tick-tocks this particular "beat" – the only object of the Temporalist world that distantly resembles a metronome. Ironically, Temporalist language (as spoken by the representatives of a theoretical elite... etc.) has no word to contain three equally spaced syllables from which musicians are able to extract the quirky temporal mode. These spoken triplets simply stop existing after a 250-270 ms threshold, and this also explains the pig that once symbolized these IOIs: that particular animal had the good habit of grunting, very much like our Western improvisers, spontaneous charges of 280-370 ms long swinish exclamations. The problem is that in contemporary Temporalist society the very access of young musicians to the farms where these animals are still bred is limited and, even if it weren't, such scholarly escapades would not solve the difficulty of discerning between the two theoretical modes. That is why the pendulum-fitted apparatus was originally invented.

J.-P.: Instrumentalists from both worlds have something in common, and that is the weakness of the fourth finger in piano players or the third in violinists. I have once read that Robert Schumann himself resorted to some quasi-inquisitorial methods in order to compensate this deficiency: he reportedly built a whole system of levers, pulleys, ropes and sand-filled purses. Well, our "metronome" represents something similar, as it is the sole concession that our ancestors made to the good tradition of assimilating the whole array of temporal modes by individual practice and actual music playing. It is still unknown why human brain refuses for a while to recognize and produce accurately this temporal mode, and this is why it sometimes has to be "grafted" to our apperception by some forcible means. If you want, the situation is somewhat similar to that experienced by the violinists who purchase a new instrument or a violin that was not played for a long period of time. They may find out that some of the sounds are amplified unsatisfactorily by the resonance box – and the only remedy for that is to bow up and down those sounds over and over again, for hours and days, until the resonance box of the instrument finally "accepts" them and starts to amplify them sufficiently.

(Summer of 2008)

My wife, who reads this book as I introduce its chapters into the hard drive of my portable Mac, says that if I really had no idea, before April the 11th, of this tedious detail from the life of violin players – then everything I am describing must not actually have been a dream. Her skepticism is heartbreaking. She has already read about sixty pages of this "extraterrestrial music theory" (her words), literally crammed with details that I obviously could not have learned before that "historical" date – and she would only allow herself to be convinced by an organologic fact that I might have known and subsequently forgotten...

About fifty years ago, Professor Schmeyer etc. was to be found in Flanders, eagerly reading a book that had just come out in the United States – in which he discovered the simplest and the most concentrated definition of accent that our scholars have ever produced: "the accent represents an event marked for the consciousness". Jean-Philippe assured me that this definition is simply perfect for the use of musicians from both shores of the enigmatic space-time that separates our civilizations.

In the discrete flow of musical time, except for the accents of intensity, all other types of accentuation that I will bring up in this chapter are subjective – that is, fabricated by means of a top-down type of perception. In other words, it is a mendacious projection of our brain that is extremely productive musically, and yet a great conspiracy of nature directed against a certain kind of knowledge to which, in the aftermath of the Brain Revolution, Temporalists started to have access.

The things I am going to describe in the following paragraphs have never been explained to me with the overt purpose of being subsequently notated in this book, and therefore I take the precaution of warning my potential readers that it is possible for me to have understood them superficially or to have erroneously translated mentally the words of a lecture dedicated to this subject that I attended during the few months in which Jean-Philippe had let me absorb Temporalist music mostly by myself.

In his world, the medical administering of a certain "altered state of consciousness" is something as common as opening a bank account in America. You just go to the psychologist responsible for your family and tell him that you wish to build a new barn in the three days remaining until the rainy season. The psychologist analyses your request and either chemically or magnetically inhibits/excites the precise nervous hubs that would make you crave to build that barn with the gusto we usually associate with sexual desire. After a few days, the effects of the cerebral optimization recede and your life goes back to "normal", enriched with a top-notch barn.

Scholars like Professor Scheinstein etc. know only too well that the illusion of accent perception may be made to disappear by means of such an optimization process. The few Temporalists who subjected themselves to this particular scientific experiment consequently related that they found it extremely hard to follow the music they were asked to listen to, because with the dissipation of accent perception all the associative faculties anent to discrete time-flow simply disappear.

The lecturer, who agreed more than once to be a subject of this experiment, and who was himself a time perception specialist, told us that musicians usually ask him "how does it feel to perceive all pulsations as non-accents?". His answer made me laugh: "Thinking that you only perceive non-accents is like supposing that a blind man only sees a dark blackness. In fact, what they perceive with their eyes is similar with the things you now see with your ears!".

And yet, "what happens to pulsations in the absence of the thesis-arsis dichotomy?" – the musicians insisted on finding out from the lecturer. "Something that exists and that may be followed only as a series of continuous temporal windows which, by the very fact of being continuous, cannot be compared", he replied. "A myriad of details that wouldn't let themselves get the shape of an entirety".

(Summer of 2008)

When I told Jean-Philippe about the lecture I had attended that day, the musician confirmed that not perceiving the thesis-arsis dichotomy is a handicap for our species, and not a blessing or the release from an illusion that impedes us from grasping the "true reality". As far as he knew, the phenomenon was associated by their psychologists with induced prosopagnosia...

...and in the next thirty minutes Jean-Philippe continued to explain to me things that I have meanwhile mostly forgotten, but which made me realize the actual amplitude of their Brain Revolution, since a mere musician (who otherwise never misses the opportunity to mock his wife for being "a psychologist, like... everybody") was able to give me a lot of expert details about such an uncommon subject. While perorating about the different kinds of induced perceptual impairments, Jean-Philippe had the typical attitude of "the Frenchman who incidentally is no expert in cheese" but, since the subject arose... amongst the monastic ones, if he were to chose between a Havarti, Munster or a Entrammes Port Salut...

From his dissertation I only remember that our musical brain's "enemy number one" is continuous time and that the thesis-arsis dichotomy represents one of the weapons used against an otherwise immaterial and unquantifiable flux of perceived sensations.

J.-P.: In our musical culture, no form of continuous time has ever been associated to something positive, or at least manageable. There is no musical composition made of *glissandi*. Besides, in both our cultures we do not have a solid psycho-musical theory for terms such as *crescendo, decrescendo, accelerando* and *rallentando*. If you ask an instrumentalist to produce a *rallentando* that is two times faster than that of his colleague, he or she wouldn't know how to produce such an augmentation and would probably improvise ineptly, since he or she has no idea as to how to tackle your request and compare one *rallentando* to another.

One day I asked Doktor Schmilowski etc. how I should write in zeuxilogic notation a *decelerando,* to which the old scholar admitted that he had no idea. In their musical semiographies too, *the discretization of continuous time* (those were his words) escaped as yet any rigorous theoretical framing. He told me that adjoining shorter and shorter musical pulsations (e.g. IOI 400-350-300-250-200-150-100 ms) is one thing (difficult, yet manageable) – while spontaneously marking out of pulsations the descending evolution of a temporal continuum is a different thing. The Professor assured me that there are countless studies treating this topic, but no one has ever proposed a viable solution that would let musicians handle the temporal continuum and add it to their professional inventory. Decades ago, Temporalists had conducted a series of experiments in which they forced the subjects to live in a "continuised" environment, in which light intensity varied permanently and perceptibly while from a series o speakers they would only hear a sonorous fluid composed of *glissandi, accelerandi, decelerandi, crescendi* and *decrescendi.* Beyond the constraints of the experiment, the life of the subjects was supposed to imitate normality, yet no subject was able to live a whole day in that environment.

As a young scholar, the Professor himself conducted a kind of scientific investigation in which he reached the conclusion that most people have experienced the worst nightmare in the form of a continuous fall into a never ending chasm.

The subject was debated for an entire evening and reached areas that had nothing to do with music: the scary sirens of police cars and ambulances, ophidiophobia (fear of snakes), the abhorrence of caterpillars, earth worms and other limbless, creeping creatures etc. The conclusion was reached that as long as our brain is able to compare, it adapts and accepts. Yet, in order to compare there must exist at least two identifiable objects of consciousness – the very thing that many continua refuse to provide. Herr Professor added that the ordinary subjective accents that we encounter in music are the consequence of the human brain's analytical and projective nature. The "thirst" for such stake-offs is so strong that illusions may take the form of some auditory figments, like the click-like sounds that may be perceived when two *glissandi* are being superimposed.

Curiously, whenever the various continua are subjected to any form of discretization, by interruptions or directional deviations, our brain generally accepts them by dispelling any kind of negative connotation. Jean-Philippe's example was the way yobs used to whistle after the Paris beauties in the working class banlieues.

Therefore, except for the dynamic accents (i.e. accents of intensity), all other types of musical accentuation are of a purely subjective nature.

73

Whenever we listen to the symmetrical tick-tack of a metronome, our top-down perception hierarchizes it in accents and non-accents, in successive ticks and tacks. All that we can do is accept the subjective rhythmization and impose an additional top-down perception by changing the former ticks in actual tacks or grouping the metronome beats in other pulsatory structures such as TH-AR-AR etc.

Once a pulsatory pattern is established, any deviation will be "marked for the consciousness". Examples abound and Jean-Philippe offered me a sample by taking a seat on the rückpositiv bench and repeatedly hitting an E-flat key in the IOI 300 ms temporal mode.

J.-P.: If this instrument were a piano, it would be easier for me to organize pulsations, for your perception, in groups of three or four, by placing a dynamic accent on the first note of each group. It was on the CASIO keyboard that I bought with Madame Richaume's pension that I discovered how musical instruments that lack the possibility for dynamic hierarchization must compensate for this drawback by means of agogic (i.e. durational) accentuation. As you may have already noticed, we do not have such instruments and this is why we seldom use this kind of accentuation, the risk being that pulsations thus marked might be regarded as false durations. What we use on a large scale are directional, dynamic and sonorous density accents.

I only later found out that Temporalist composers (in scores) and interpreters (spontaneously) have the habit of materializing ambiguous accents as small clusters meant to dispel, at the level of audience perception, any misrepresentation of the correct TH-AR hierarchy:

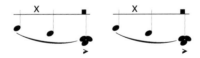

In this simple example, the composer has notated an anacrusical AR-AR-TH relationship that has an unusual descending profile. The deeply rooted Temporalist tradition of performing such prosodical structures as ascending successions of sounds led to the existence of a strong apperceptual expectation, from the three note group, to form a metacrusical TH-AR-AR structure. This is why the actual accent must be stressed by means of other "markings for consciousness", these including the small clusters illustrated above that I stumbled upon quite often in the scores of a few composers who, if not from such a different world, would have been comparable with Johannes Brahms.

Perhaps this is the place to briefly describe the uncanny cultural differences that separate our musicians and music lovers from Jean-Philippe's fellow citizens.

At the end of our long meetings in his drawing room, the old Doktor pointed out to me that there would be two things that I wouldn't be able to export, no matter the effort, to France. The first one is the complex relationship between the temporal nature of their spoken language and the structuring of pulsations in Temporalist music. This relationship is as subtle (yet apparent) as: the accents preceded by long anacrusical passages in the Baroque French Ouverture – and the French language itself; the German idiom and the march-like rhythms present in most symphonies by Gustav Mahler; or Hungarian language and Bela Bartók's "inverted" dotted rhythms:

The other thing the immaterial customs office that separates the two worlds will surely confiscate is the cultural baggage that every Temporalist possesses, and which contains an impressive apperceptive background over which their music is always contextualized, within a broad historical frame and depending on each individual's elective affinities. As initially Jean-Philippe found it hard to link classical European music he was listening to with the Harmony schoolbooks' precepts, as well as with his own perception, he was not spared certain frustrations and depressions in his "expat" life. At some point he told me that back then he was utterly unable to understand why the perfect fourth was presented in those Harmony or Counterpoint manuals as a dissonant interval – since his ear could not perceive any tension upon listening to it. The same way, to him the diminished seventh chord is even today "a dissonant yet *extremely stable* chord" while the augmented triad is "both consonant and stable, as it is composed only of consonant intervals".

When he recognizes them in European classical music, Jean-Philippe actually *is* able to perceive them as alien from the type of stability provided by the predominant and alternating major and minor chords – and understands theoretically why the mentioned chords were considered to be dissonant *in this particular context*. What he is unable to understand is why the E flat–G natural major third is considered by us to be gay and luminous in countless possible contexts, while somber and menacing in this particular configuration:

Many such cultural exceptions will probably never leave the world that created them. As for me, I still do not understand why, for instance, the third pulsation in a group of four, in the IOI 100 ms temporal mode, is not considered in Temporalist schoolbooks as a secondary accent. I also was, for a long period of time, unable to understand how there can exist AR values that are not placed in any relationship with a TH value etc.

I am glad that I made this short trip in the realm of the culturally based incompatibilities because the following type of accentuation does not exist in Temporalist music – and Jean-Philippe, although a Parisian by adoption, while understanding its theoretical framework, cannot perceive it. I refer to a prosodical accent of a peculiar nature that we mostly encounter in cliché-laden gestural musical genres, such as waltzes. Indeed, the "ram-pam-pam" ostinato establishes a TH-AR-AR pattern in which the accent is of a metrical nature – which is non-existent in Temporalist musical culture (or, better said, it exists but in a very different shape). Jean-Philippe is able to follow quite well the metrical accents of European music yet what he is unable to understand is the very "survival" of this accent in our perception when, for instance, before an instrumental cadenza, the tempo gets loose due to a *molto ritardando* indication. In such contexts, the time interval between the three pulsations of the "ram-pam-pam" formula may get prolonged up to two or three seconds:

It was a fascinating experience for me to find out that our beautiful metrical hierarchization, which I had previously considered to be something natural to any kind of music, may be regarded as something exotic for a Temporalist ear. I will return to this "exoticism" after a few lines about the last type of accentuation discussed in the house of Doktor Schleverkühn etc. – the syncopation accent.

A difference that could not pass unnoticed while comparing our classical composers with their maestros is that, in the absence of the metrical system, listeners' projective expectations are more reduced in their tradition. We are used to think that a musical composition that starts out in a certain tempo and bears a certain time signature should continue at the given pace until the end. Such things are inconceivable in classical Temporalist music and for this reason anticipatory projectiveness and "the rule of good continuation" have different connotations in the two cultures. The same way even expectation thwarting differs. For instance, in our tradition, an eighth note in a 4/4 measure that is suspended over the bar line creates one of the possible syncopation types. Our brain takes notice that the law which says the first beat of the second measure should be materialized is infringed upon, and "marks the exception for the consciousness", which in turn makes the previously unaccented sixth note be perceived as an accent. The Professor told me that the unaccented eighth note does not "take over" the accent of the following beat, because the AR value becomes a TH only after the bar line, when the exception is detected at the level of our anticipatory perception. That is roughly how this kind of accentuation works. In fact, the cognitive processing of syncopations substantially differs, depending on the actual length of the notes involved and the perceptual thresholds that define these durations.

Temporalist composers know only too well how this differentiated phenomenology functions and, as such, use syncopations in compositional contexts that are specific to every IOI. They also notate the dual nature (i.e. an AR that becomes a TH) of this kind of pulsation, by slurring the two values:

Just as it was hard for Jean-Philippe to understand why our educated perception labels the augmented triad as unstable harmonically, I discovered that two years were not enough for me to perceive the IOI 133 ms temporal mode as "false", "exotic" or "unstable". I deduced it from the compound division of a IOI 400 ms beat:

For most Temporalists, the resulted mode is an old IOI 120 ms that is lousily performed by an unskilled musician. To me it was and still is one of the possible isochronous tempi. Herr Schlangfarben etc. couldn't refrain from covering his ears when I performed the D major *Prelude* in this particular temporal mode. I was equally unable to ignore Jean-Philippe's grimace – at least I expected more understanding from him, as he was lengthily exposed, while in Paris, to the homicidal attack of such isochronies…

That was the only moment when I experienced a nervous breakdown. My dialogue with Jean-Philippe, who laughed and shouted at the same time (in order to cover my avalanche of interrogations), went roughly like this:

Me: What's so hard in taking a bloody pulsation and splitting it into three equal parts?

J.-P.: Why don't you split, then, a perfect fourth into three equal intervals?

Me: It's not the same thing!

J.-P.: Oh, yes it is!

Me: Fine! But why don't you add up two pulsations in order to obtain an augmented temporal mode?

J.-P.: Well, that is something that we do, but you have to be patient until we get to this subject.

I finally allowed myself to be convinced that the innumerable hours spent by my guide in the company of Temporalist music have modelled his perception in such a way that any temporal mode that breaks the just noticeable difference (JND) accepted for any given "tempered" IOI (or for the old modes) – is automatically considered as "false". It is probably for a similar reason that I find it impossible for me to intonate any of the Indian movie tunes sung by Aishwarya Rai, although, much to my wife's despair, I like listening to them. It seems that the tempered chromatic scale has equally dug into my brain a grid that catalogues pitches in a unique way that now operates as a second nature by censoring the assimilation of other, distant, sonorous systems. For the Temporalists who first listen to an excerpt of our music, "everything sounds the same", no matter if the sample is from a Haydn quartette or from *La Marseillaise*. They would initially hear a combination of "false" temporal modes that is tediously repeating itself while accompanied by a bizarre sonorous fabric that Temporalists define as "elaborate", although they feel unable to follow its evolution. One day, Jean-Philippe, who is the Grand Master of Comparisons, told me:

J.-P.: Hmm… untempered, "false" intervals, repetitious melodic structures, quite minimalist… I guess that before I formed my harmonic hearing, European music was, *mutatis mutandis*, similar to what you feel while listening to a Gamelan jegog ensemble!

I remember that for a while I was quite intrigued by their initial ("all our music sounds the same") impression, but Jean-Philippe gave me something to think about when he explained to me that in their language the equivalent for *sonorité* is *temporalité* and that from *this* point of view our music may seem at first a little bit indistinct. With a quite surprising exception: there are certain Baroque Fugues, especially from The Well Tempered Clavier, that Temporalists can almost follow.

I was told that the lady whom I first saw performing that Messiaen composition the day I was "imported" actually knows by heart all these Fugues and, after the expensive and time-consuming cloning of that Olof Granfeldt piano, she was able to perform them in both the Temporalist manner and in the "bizarre" tempi regularly chosen by our pianists and harpsichordists. On the poster announcing a concert that I actually attended to while still living in Herr Schalieri's etc. house, one could read the following:

Madame Temporalissima
Demonstrative concert of "Music made of sounds"
performed on the copy of an original instrument
8 versions of a famous composition
written by a very appreciated composer

While reading aloud this announcement, Jean-Philippe pierced me with an ironic look because I was laughing at the fact that Temporalist language is unable to transcribe, black on white, the name of Johann Sebastian Bach.

In fact, at that concert "Madame Temporalissima" (as I dubbed her) only performed the first fugue, in C major, from the first Book of The Well Tempered Clavier. Before attacking the first note she was kind enough to make a short introduction (of which I did not understand a jot since I was not yet "linguistically optimized") in which she repeated over and over again, in "our language", Bach's name, so that the public perceive the reiteration of the same group of vowels and consonants. Amusing...

(Summer of 2008)

My wife seems to be equally amused. After getting a degree in public relations, she was proud to have adopted the good habit of storing in her memory, after a loud pronunciation, the names of all people she would meet during the various meetings and business dinners. Her colleagues were amazed by her associative memory. If she is unable to grasp a name at the first attempt, she would insist that the respective person repeat his or her name and produce a business card. Problems started to appear in the mid 1980s, when the company she was then working for decided to externalize their production lines in the South-East Pacific emerging countries. Now the new business partners would present themselves by shelling Simone with a combination of short and bizarre syllables which she, as she was accustomed to do in such cases, tried to repeat. The reactions from the Oriental guests were quite baffling. Once, a lady got upset because in her imagination my wife must have been born in Indochina and raised by local nannies – or else how could she pronounce with such a vernacular zest the Vietnamese equivalent for "twisted legs"?

At first, Madame Temporalissima performed the Fugue in a purely Temporalist manner, so that the sixteenth notes perfectly matched the IOI 200 ms mode, the eighth notes the IOI 400 ms mode while the thirty-second notes, the IOI 100 ms mode. The audience seemed to me genuinely interested, especially because even the intervals sounded to them quite familiar, as the sixteenth notes have in general a step-by-step profile while the eighth notes from the subject outline at some point a series of successive leaps:

Some of the listeners nodded approvingly after which, in a bout of excessive vanity, the piano player taught them how to applaud (our way, and without too much success) and moved forward to the second version of the same Fugue, not before repeating three times Wanda Landowska's name. I was unable to sense any apparent difference between the first tempo and the second, yet there was mumbling in the audience and I could hear both assenting and dissatisfied grunts (at least these are identical in the two worlds) while the macédoine of reactions was a spectacle in itself: curiosity mixed with amusement, surprise and bafflement. In the end, Jean-Philippe, who was sitting next to me, whispered into my ear that this time the sixteenth note was outlining a "false" temporal mode, at around IOI 220 ms. After that, the pianist presented us larger and larger tempi "created" by Keith Jarrett, Kenneth Gilbert, Glenn Gould, Davitt Moroney, Sviatoslav Richter and Friedrich Gulda. The last performance was in fact greeted with a few angry vociferations. Jean-Philippe wrote for me into the air the approximate value of the sixteenth notes: four-two-zero. IOI 420 ms! More than double in comparison to Landowska's version. All in all, to me, that short demonstrative concert constituted an important lesson, as it showed me how culturally different two human communities can be.

Jean-Philippe did not miss the opportunity to produce one of his ever surprising comparisons. As soon as we returned home, my bald friend hurriedly picked up one of the writing tools scattered all around the dining room and, as I was continuing to share with him my recent impressions, he started to scribble something at Herr Professor's desk. After a short while he shouted "Voilà!" and stormed the rückpositiv waving a piece of paper in his right hand. Here is what he was so keen to play for me:

J.-P.: To our ears, "twice as fast" is not just another tempo – it is a completely different music! If our pianist had doubled all the pitch intervals of the fugue while preserving the first tempo, nobody in the audience would have protested – except for you. You would have said something like "what on Earth is this nonsense"?

This mode ends the series of primary modes for which the Temporalist curriculum imposes that students assimilate them through the mechanisms of absolute memory. When Jean-Philippe first uttered the words "primary modes" I started to count them and was consequently amused to find out that they are precisely seven, like the steps of our old diatonic scale. Perhaps if I were a Cabalist, such coincidences might have seemed quite interesting to me.

IOI 400 ms also coincides with a strong perceptual threshold that is defined by a series of psychophysical phenomena. Professor Schöndon etc. pointed out to me that, in our culture, the 400 ms long beat (MM = 150) is the first that allows for binary *sub*-divisions, each lasting 100 ms. This is one of the reasons most musicians of the Old Continent and the New World consider this time-span as beat-specific, whereas for IOI 350 ms the general view is that its pulsations may still be considered to be the divisions of a (700 ms long) beat.

Yet, for Temporalists such classifications do not make too much sense. In their psycho-musical world, the IOI 400 ms temporal mode is defined by the fact that, finally, from one pulsation to the next, attention may be shifted sustainably, for undetermined periods of time. The rate of this particular attention transfer, I was told, is by no means comfortable, as IOI 600 ms is in fact the first temporal mode that allows for a *complete* and unforced attention shift. Jean-Philippe, who while waiting for my otherworldly delivery became an encyclopedia of comparisons, told me that IOI 600 ms is like a normal, average human walk (about 5 feet per second), whereas IOI 400 ms is perceived by our brain very much like a "forced march" that will surely be more demanding physically – yet sustainable for long periods of time.

(Summer of 2008)
I think that it is this "physical condition" which distinguishes an athlete from a sedentary person. In the case of the IOI 400 ms timespan, the arbitrary and continuous attention transfer from one pulsation to the next does not come in handy for beginner instrumentalists, who perceive this psychophysical threshold at around IOI 430-440 ms. Professionals, though – who have spent thousands of hours learning and trying to optimally allot their attention from one pulsatory group to another – have developed those neuronal circuits that now help them project an even, analytical perception over each 400 ms long pulsation.

"The maximum rate of sustainable attention shift", as it is called, is thus a perceptual threshold whose placement differs from one individual to another and that shrinks its specific durations depending on the "neuronal condition" of any given musician. Most people, I was told, manage to transfer their attention continuously and evenly once every 400-440 milliseconds whenever they are asked to do that "as fast as they can".

I asked Herr Schlippendeutsch etc. how they can determine these values, and his answer was:

– Oh, that is easy: by performing the pentagram test!

Upon telling me that, our host took a piece of paper and drew this zigzag on it:

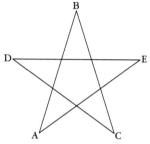

Herr Sch. etc.: You must concentrate on the small pentagon in the middle, so that you encompass visually the A, B, C, D and E angles on an equal footing. Then you have to follow their succession mentally, without moving your eyes around, faster and faster and taking great care that the resulting pulsations do not hierarchize in prosodical combinations of TH and AR values:

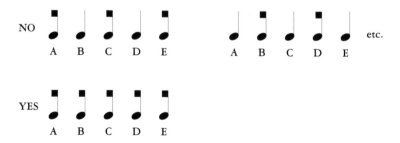

– You may tap lightly with one finger the fastest succession you will be able to get to, he added.

I did just that and after a short while I observed that the rate at which I was transferring my attention from one angle to another stabilized in a kind of fast "motor rhythm". My repeated attempts to quicken the tempo without hierarchizing mentally the pulsations thus obtained failed each time. A few seconds after I started to tap my finger, Jean-Philippe stopped me and informed me that, in temporal perception psychology, a pulsatory structure that a subject is able to repeat for three seconds is considered to be indefinitely sustainable. (I hope that I will find a place in this book to comment upon this approximately three second long temporal window that we may find often times in the structuring of our composers' musical phrases.)

The result? IOI 410 ms in Jean-Philippe's estimation. He also assured me that, if I keep the pentagram at hand and repeat the experiment several times daily, in less than a month I would make a first step into the world of Temporalist musical professionalization.

– How come my result was so good?

– You probably are an experienced sight reader, Jean-Philippe replied. That is an excellent exercise for the optimization of the attention shift rate.

Indeed, whereas my piano technique declined steadily in the last three decades, the sole consolation was the fact that each evening I used to sight read from the hundreds of scores that I inherited from my mother or collected over the years. Sometimes I would do that for five hours in a row, or even more.

From a musical point of view, the first implication of the sustainable transfer of attention is that we finally can "look a metronome in the eye" and force ourselves to perceive its pulsations unhierarchized as "ticks" and "tocks". Temporalist schoolbooks claim that every 400 ms long arbitrary attention transfer that is repeated for more than three seconds transforms the respective pulsations in as many separate accents. The truth is that I have rarely seen the corresponding notation in the various Temporalist musical scores…

…but I have many times encountered prosodically hierarchized structures:

Jean-Philippe did not miss the opportunity to remind me of my recent nervous outburst and inform me that, in the case of this temporal mode, Temporalist musicians tolerate relative or associative memorization. In other words, those who have not assimilated properly the IOI 400 ms temporal mode may *initially* devise it as the augmentation of the IOI 200 ms mode. Unexperienced instrumentalists use the following trick:

But they are not allowed to continue it like this:

Herr Professor explained to me that in their musical tradition 1/2 is not the same as 2/4 or 4/8. A duration that was obtained by means of a mental process of division or augmentation automatically expels the respective duration from the psychophysical determinants that previously made it relevant from a musical point of view. For instance, if their students were taught that IOI 400 ms is in fact the augmentation of the IOI 200 ms mode, they would never perform the first beat-specific isochrony where attention transfer becomes sustainable, but an inertial, "divisional" mode whose pulsations are slurred two by two.

Dr. Sch. etc.: A 20 karat crystal cut in two and glued together again will never be for sale as a 20 karat crystal, but as a montage made of two 10 karat crystals.

Hitherto I had thought that only Jean-Philippe was good with comparisons...

The seven primary modes constitute the daily bread of all Temporalist musicians. I never actually counted, but the incidence of these durations in comparison with longer ones is clearly larger in their musical literature. For this reason, apart from a few insipid contemporary scores, in the two years spent far away from my Parisian home, I never listened to anything that might have resembled a *largo*. In their tradition, the idea of reverie is associated with repetitiveness and the confirmation of musical expectations. I actually liked the frisky, alert appearance of Temporalist music, although sometimes I missed the sound of a dying chord, in *pianissimo*.

Seen by many as the comfortable version of the IOI 400 ms mode, IOI 450 is the first isochrony that Temporalists do not feel compelled to assimilate by means of absolute memorization. This is because IOI 450 ms is not considered to belong to the group of primary modes, as it opens the series of compound modes. IOI 450 ms is deduced *first* by means of a rhythmical artifice that is so known to us – the addition of three durations taken over from IOI 150 ms:

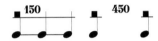

Whenever interpreters feel awkward to access directly the specific pace of the IOI 450 ms mode, they are free to resort to this augmentative strategy – while knowing that the first compound mode has in fact its own character, that shouldn't be altered other than in cases of absolute necessity. Jean-Philippe assured me that *all* contemporary Temporalist virtuosi actually had this mode assimilated and stored into the inventory of their absolute memory. Some musicologists are even of the opinion that had there been an historical bias for compound modes (i.e. between IOI 450 ms and IOI 700 ms), musicians would have assimilated them all by means of the same absolute memorization mechanisms that they use in the case of primary modes.

In the chapter that I will dedicate to "passages" (a kind of pulsatory modulations) I will be able to better explain why most interpreters prefer to devise the first duration of a IOI 450 ms mode by joining together a 200 ms long pulsation and a 250 ms long pulsation (not necessarily in this order). The idea is that a IOI 150 ms long pulsation is too distant to constitute the basis for deducing the IOI 450 ms timespan: the former's strong inertial character is considered to infringe upon the latter's isochrony, which is characterized by some very different psychoperceptual phenomena. The juxtaposition of two timespans, IOI 200 ms and IOI 250 ms, that at least are placed beyond the minimal acton threshold, seems to settle an acceptable compromise, at least in the eyes of Temporalist musicians. As for me, I wonder how I could notate this bizarre aksak in our musical notation:

As I expected, beginners devise the IOI 500 ms temporal mode by adding up two pulsations taken over from IOI 250 ms, while professionals who were unable to assimilate it thoroughly cannot conceive to devise it in other way but as a 300 ms + 200 ms (or 200 ms + 300 ms) juxtaposition. The reasons are similar to those explained in the previous chapter (i.e. the 200 ms + 250 ms addition).

I asked Jean-Philippe where this obsession for avoiding musical beats came from in their culture, as in our music beat is one of the most important rhythmical concepts. The fact that in their interpretative tradition IOI 450 ms and IOI 500 ms are preferentially derived from the addition of two different timespans did not seem to me to be a matter of mere "diversity", but something extremely artificial, a cerebral contrivance created, in my inexpert view, in spite of some obvious ecological tendencies and in spite of the way our brain is programmed to hierarchize durations. As I was already anticipating his reply, I asked Jean-Philippe to avoid telling me again that we do not necessarily associate the octave with the juxtaposition of two tritones or the perfect fifth with two adjoining major-minor (moll-dur) thirds. Here is his reply, as I was able to recall it after almost two years:

J.-P.: My dear friend, everything is vibration and we are nothing more than a huge factory of perceptions that help us live and survive in this multiform thicket of external stimuli. If you speak to a physicist, you might find out that matter itself may be reduced to the ubiquitous vibrations referred to in your world by those who study the String Theory. Give me your hand and convince yourself that the body that you posses now actually perceives this matter, as it does the body you left in Paris. The colors that you see with your eyes are but a small segment in this huge vibrational universe, situated in between the Gamma radiations, X-rays and ultra violets on one end and infrareds, microwaves and radio waves on the other. The civilization that you come from is simply obsessed about appropriating all these physical realities and this is why I am sure you know what I am talking about. Well, somewhere in between infrasounds and ultrasounds Nature bestowed upon us a sound detecting organ, the ears, and several brain areas dedicated to the processing of sonorous stimuli. I have no idea why, but your culture developed a special kind of sensitivity for this perceptual segment. We can only suppose that it was thus enhanced because of the phonetical nature of your spoken languages. It was quite a shock for the generation of my parents to find out that there is a parallel world in which people understand each other even if they speak with strikingly differing pulsatory patterns, yet become incomprehensible if they change the "mere" sounds that their words are composed of. The same way, in between the lowest vibration that we may still perceive as sound and the first temporal mode that allows for rhythmization – that is, around IOI 83 ms in ternary grouping – there is to be found the only segment in which our brain perceives vibrations as… actual vibrations, by creating the *crepitus* sensation. It seems that none of our civilizations ever developed a learned sensitivity for this segment, which does not imply that other, parallel human civilizations did not. Finally, in between IOI 100 ms and IOI 700 ms, humans have developed a strong control over pulsations' isochronicity, that is, by direct perception. As you might have observed, we are particularly competent in the small area ranging between IOI 100 ms and IOI 400 ms. Our language managed to cope with a myriad of significations by means of some "untempered" spoken pulsations lasting from approximately 70 ms to approximately 320 ms, exceptions aside… You don't want to know how our local ranger speaks when he is drunk and insists to explain to whoever is listening why he respects women… Between IOI 700 ms and IOI 1000 ms the direct perception of pulsations' isochronicity gradually weakens and we can start to speak of "estimation" – another modality by which our brain assesses isochronicity, that becomes a necessity for pulsations lasting 1000 ms or more. The idea is that when IOIs go beyond 2000 ms per pulsation we become unable even to *compare* pulsations directly as, in principle, each such pulsation will occupy a distinct temporal window. It is like trying to compare two individuals placed one at your back and one facing you, so that you will have to turn your head to and fro in order to compare them. *Mutatis mutandis*, just before circa IOI 2000 ms, the two individuals are placed at the lateral limits of your peripheral vision. If I'm not wrong, in your psychology schoolbooks this kind of comparative perception is governed by something called "the law of proximity". At about 3 seconds and beyond, it becomes improper even to speak of pulsations. Such time spans are defined by us as perceptual cycles. While in Paris, I had the opportunity to read several studies confirming the fact that verses or hemistichs in rhymed poetry last about 2.7 seconds; approximately 3 seconds define the length of many musical motifs, groups of motifs or half-phrases from the Viennese Classicism. I can assure you that our music too contains an awful lot of pulsatory groups which are born and die out in about 3 seconds, but I'm afraid I don't know if we have a clear explanation for the recurrence of this time-span: it seems to be the natural rhythm for the absorption and processing of chunks of information that is specific for short-term memory. And now, returning to the main idea: if everything may be reduced to vibrations then sounds, crepitus-like vibrations and pulsations can therefore be construed as just as many phases of a single phenomenon that is grasped differently by our senses. As concerns the interpretation of vibrations, between my world and yours there is an additional barrier. If you want, we are the Eskimos who will always say that water is melted snow, while you will consider that ice is solidified water. Similarly, to us pitches are pulsations that are too fast to be used as such, while for you isochronous pulsations are perhaps sounds that are just too low to be perceived by the human ear. At least that's what I understood from an article written by a famous contemporary German composer, entitled *...How Time Passes...* These being said, the double or the half of a given frequency *is always another step* in the vast scale of vibrations. In sounds, we experience the jump to another octave while in temporal modes theory we witness a radical change in the perceptual phenomenology anent to the respective – halved or doubled – IOIs. Just think about it: at IOI 50 ms we deal with the *crepitus* sensation, at IOI 100 ms, the double of the previous value, we encounter the binary threshold of subjective rhythmization, while at IOI 200 ms pops in the minimal acton threshold. Furthermore, at IOI 400 ms we think of the first sustainable rate of attention shift. Finally, at IOI 800 ms we can already feel the presence of the "temporal gap" sensation, and at IOI 1600 ms we need to start assessing the effects of the proximity law – only to witness at around IOI 3200 ms the transformation of pulsations into perceptual cycles.

After this long dissertation I had almost forgotten where our discussion actually started from. But Jean-Philippe had not. He insisted that I do not transcribe into this book his *ab ovo* generalizations and better focus only on the aesthetic reasons by which Temporalists refuse to think of pulsations as durational divisions or augmentations.

J.-P.: In our Temporal Harmony treatises there is a precept called "the avoidance of double cyclicity". It looks quite similar to "the avoidance of parallel fifths" that I learned about in all your old Tonal Harmony books. What I mean is that neither double cyclicity nor the parallel fifths necessarily "sound bad". They are only refuted, on strictly aesthetic grounds, by the stylistic habits of their corresponding traditions. Soon, when you will be able to follow our musical scores, you will surely note that isochronous pulsations are most times grouped so that they do not create pulsatory cycles at the level of their immediate augmentation:

In order to achieve that, our classical composers used a whole inventory of compositional techniques, the simplest being by distributing unevenly the TH values, by varying the prosodical relationships (i.e. anacrusical, metacrusical and combined) and the durations. You see, at *this* level, our tradition discourages repetitiveness – as we are prone to consider it tedious. While in Paris, I once entered an underground club for a quick espresso only to find myself plunged into a house music shrine! After two minutes I felt like going nuts! What kind of imbecile could enjoy something like that? Well, returning to compound temporal modes and their division… avoiding the double cyclicity applies here as well. If we were to split constantly 500 ms in two halves of 250 ms each, we would obtain two temporal modes…

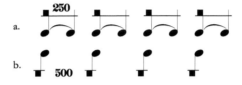

…which in Temporal Harmony schoolbooks is depicted as a typical example of the double cyclicity (IOI 250 ms and IOI 500 ms) that has to be avoided at all costs. Why? An old school musicologist would tell you: "because it sounds bad". A Temporalist musician like myself, who knows so many things about the bar-rhythmical system, would rather say that double and even triple cyclicity does not represent a nuisance as long as the interest is focused on individual pitches and harmonic progressions. If he were not busy with his academic duties right now, Herr Professor would have told you that, in the case of double cyclicity, the perceptual attributes of *both* interacting temporal modes are being altered. Yet, I prefer to pass on to you the bewilderment of a child who once attended one of the demonstrative concerts of our pianist, who played Robert Schumann's *Toccata* opus 7: "Mommy, but… in this music… what is it that the interpreter has to do?" To him, the countless measures that displayed one single temporal mode looked like an extremely boring toy. And now, the grand finale… There was a period in my French life when I was sent to spy on the researchers and composers affiliated with IRCAM. I then tried to see whether there could be an immediate benefit for our music in cybernetics and whether we should invent for ourselves computers and software to help musicians in their creative struggle with pulsations. I remember a series of long discussions with a handful of young researchers and the conclusion that I reached was that, as far as we are concerned, those sophisticated machines wouldn't serve us well since terms such as anacrusical, *crepitus*, subjective rhythmization, temporal gap, pulsatory inertia etc. – in the absence of which the rationalization of our music theory wouldn't be possible – are unquantifiable. All these phenomena are not intrinsic to the IOIs that carry them to our senses, but to our perception itself – and I assume that computers cannot be programmed to simulate perceptions and have the temporal competence that is only specific to the human brain. At the same time, superimposed cyclicities, so typical for the bar-rhythmical system, are perfectly quantifiable, and as such your computers get along with them so well. But… *dove è la musica?* I saw more than once French students practicing while reading the newspaper or talking over their handsfree telephones: that is something unimaginable in our more elaborate music, as reproducing those intricate discrete time structures ceaselessly employs our cognitive functions. In our music, you will see, automatization takes place at another level. Well, the main difference between the temporalities of our musical traditions rests in the refusal versus the abuse of the double or triple etc. cyclicity. This is why we do not split the IOI 500 ms pulsations right in the middle!

I assume that, if Jean-Philippe's demonstration were a legal case, the defendant would have been acquitted. As for me, I remained quite skeptical, although the words of my guide made sense – as long as we do not go beyond the Temporalist music paradigm. It was only later that I accepted fully the incommensurability of our traditions, namely on the day I found out that their music was never associated with dance movements. Temporalists do not dance! Their youngsters, although extremely libertine sexually, do not couple by means of such mating rituals. They do have some choreographic pageants created by composers specialised in what Temporalists call "the visual mode of music", in which sounds are replaced by corporal motions adapted for a certain theatrical purpose. Most times the movements are doubled or counterpointed by sounds in impressive mega shows resembling remotely what we call dance-theatre, contemporary dance or even break dancing.

Now I regret that I never asked why the double cyclicity avoidance becomes less mandatory in inertial temporal modes such as IOI 100 ms and IOI 150 ms. Their classical scores display a great choice of such structures during whose performance their instrumentalists too could read a newspaper. Quite a mystery…

My fingers ache after a whole day in which I did nothing else but write. Tomorrow is Sunday and I think of getting outside at least for an hour, although the walk will surely be spoiled by the many thoughts that claim their turn to be put on paper. My wife looks quite baffled by my sudden outburst of creativity. At the moment she is quiet, perhaps waiting for me to make the first explanatory step…

THE COMPOUND TEMPORAL MODES
IOI 550 MS, IOI 600 MS AND IOI 650 MS

(Sunday, April the 13th, 2008)

A new day for me and a topic that has already been introduced: compound modes. It will not come therefore as a surprise that Temporalists mentally compose the commencement of these isochronies in the following manner:

IOI 550 ms — 300 ms + 250 ms (or 350 ms + 200 ms), or vice versa
IOI 600 ms — 350 ms + 250 ms, or vice versa
IOI 650 ms — 350 ms + 300 ms, or vice versa

This mental elogization of the modes' first pulsations is performed whenever interpreters are not sure that they can handle either the isochronicity of the respective IOI or the accurate duration of a solitary pulsation. In all other situations, these compound modes are thought of as rows of equal pulsations, the same way primary modes are. There was one thing that I did not understand: since IOI 400 ms is considered to be a primary mode, why is never used in any of the above mental additions? Why, for instance, IOI 650 ms is not initially built up as 400 ms + 250 ms? Jean-Philippe explained to me that the main reason why IOI 400 ms is regarded as a primary mode is the following: it may be quite easily assimilated and introduced into the inventory of absolute memorization and, as such, it does not require to be thought of initially as the sum of two smaller and uneven time-spans (e.g. 250 ms + 150 ms), although the practice is still tolerated for beginners who ceased deducing it augmentatively (i.e. as 200 + 200 ms). If we ignore all that, IOI 400 ms has the characteristics of a composed mode and as such its specific duration is never used for the mental elogization of the IOI 650 ms, yet tolerated for the initial buildup of larger temporal modes.

Today, after having looked through literally hundreds of Temporalist scores, I can tell that all compound modes, from IOI 450 ms to IOI 700 ms, had an important, yet secondary, role to play (with the small exception of vocal music, which in that world is only characterized by its extreme paucity).

By the time a kind of pulsatory polyphony of pulsatory voices was all the rage in Temporalist musical composition, the durations specific to compound modes often times became the pulsatory background upon which primary modes would evolve. Later on, compound modes became a kind of supportive texture supposed to "resonate" in accordance with the events taking place at faster pulsatory levels. It has been only in the last seventy or so years that composers started to bring these modes into the foreground and the public to get used to the idea, although most concertgoers still consider that bizarre.

– Concerti for tuba and orchestra are not too popular in your world either, Jean-Philippe ineptly commented.

Sometimes I felt that some of his comparisons were meant to be only understood by himself. I could only deduce that, to Temporalists, compound modes represent a kind of low register destined to support the compositional plots taking place at the level of the faster primary modes.

The first Temporalist "singers" appeared spontaneously in the backstages of concert halls, during the ad-hoc student gatherings, on the lawns of the music schools and universities or… in the shower. Whenever an instrumentalist felt the need to materialize some pulsatory structures in the absence of his or her musical instrument, the voice would become the last resort. For this reason, most of their vocal performers imitate the timbre and tuning of a real instrument – but few are able to match the latter's technical capabilities. For this reason, human voice is used in Temporalist contemporary music like a kind of exotic instrument, while the art of singing is not in the curriculum of any of their universities.

In the last two or three months of my stay there I was sporadically introduced to the underground world of Temporalist music and I enjoyed a short yet wonderful bohemian experience along with a bunch of uninhibited students whom, in the absence of Jean-Philippe, I used to cheer up by singing all the interbellum hits that I learned from my mother. No one knew why, but my voice seemed to stir up the youngsters who in turn would accompany me, imitating my crooning. A rooster farm heralding the dawn over a pasture populated with mooing cows, neighboring the Big City's knackery and the porcine slaughterhouse at the hour when church bells produce those ultrasounds that make dogs remember that they are related to wolves. I forgot to mention that the church was on fire and countless fire engines were wailing their sirens. Indeed, there actually were such unforgettable moments.

(Summer of 2008)
The shortness of this chapter broke my heart, so I decided to move here a page that I initially placed at the end of the temporal modes presentation.

One day, Jean-Philippe told me that all comparisons between our musical worlds that he was so expertly making were not the result of an arbitrary decision, but the way he, as a Temporalist musician, was able to appropriate "the Art of Sounds". In other words, comparisons appeared out of sheer necessity.

He initially discovered that both our melodies and harmonic verticalizations are closely linked to the intonational capabilities of the human voice – of which he was not aware at that time. Given these circumstances, he started to listen to recorded lieder, choirs, cantatas and operas, trying to sing along this or that melodic line. The first results were a disaster, but my friend comforted himself with the thought that a European musician too, first encountering Temporalist music, would find it extremely difficult to synchronize his or her tapping with its intricate temporal structures.

Starting out from this self-consolation, Jean-Philippe decided that he should learn solfeggio and that the first necessary step in this direction was the accurate intonation of the twelve temperate intervals within an octave. He obviously thought that these intervals represent roughly what temporal modes are in the Temporalist musical tradition. Both are learned – or "assimilated" – initially, in a separate manner. The same way, in the coming years, modulations were compared to pulsatory passages while dynamic harmony, produced by the polyphonic movement of voices – with the pulsatory groupings. And so on…

J.-P.: I had reached the conclusion that our musical worlds, although incommensurable, may be reduced to a kind of common denominator if one consents that the key-question is "what would I associate that with?". André, for instance, what would you associate a minor third with? And, while answering, think of the chasm that exists between your brain and that of my wife's, who does not associate this interval with anything at all!

Without too much thought, I replied that I may associate the minor third (or the augmented tone, for that matter) with: minor tonalities; one of the intervals that compose the major, minor and diminished triads; the major seventh chord and the diminished seventh chord; 1001 musical compositions; its twelve possible "incarnations"; the fourth, the fifth and the sixth overtones; pien-tones; the major sixth; some extended chords; three consecutive semitones; enharmonic modulation… even with the flat, double flat and the double sharp symbols…

J.-P.: Now, tell me… Before coming here, what did you associate with the isochronies placed at around IOI 200 ms?

That was one tough question, indeed. Of course, I unconsciously associated them with a myriad of musical compositions that contained them in one of the relevant temporal strata, but I was unable to name one on the spot. As I had already assimilated the respective mode in its "temperate" version, I played it in my head for a while and then whispered, slightly embarrassed:

– With *allegretto?*

The use of pulsations as musical rests is a common place in Temporalist scores. In their tradition there are actually two kinds of such intermissions: structural rests and interruptions. The former stand on equal footing with any other pulsation – it is just that they are not materialized as sounds. Instrumentalists know how to "perform" them either by pressing their fingers against some "blank" (or false) keys specially manufactured, in the air or, finally, in stringed instruments, pressing the string without making it vibrate. The important thing is that the respective pulsations be formally performed, but without any sonorous materialization.

I recall a beautiful contemporary composition for three wind instruments entitled "Lines without contour". The author had marked all TH pulsations in the score as structural rests:

As the composer happened to be a specialist in subjective accentuation theory, he knew from the outset which performed pulsations will be perceived as perceptual accents by listeners and speculated masterfully the latter's poetics. All in all, what I know is that "Lines without contour" is one of the few contemporary Temporalist compositions that I would like to listen again to. Upon returning home (at that point I lived in an apartment offered to us by a wealthy university), Jean-Philippe offered to introduce me to a new book. I replied that, at least for a couple of hours, I wanted to lay down and muse, because I had just listened to a masterpiece!

Obviously, not only TH values can be (im)materialized as rests. AR pulsations may be performed in a similar way:

Jean-Philippe told me that, decades ago, there was a whole trend in which certain composers tried to develop the poetics of structural rests.

Their concerts were attended by many interpreters who were curious to see how that music sounded when you are not performing it, since the differences (i.e. performer vs. listener) in this case are quite apparent. For a musical culture that was hitherto used to rendering evident in any possible way the TH-AR dichotomy, the fact that there was a new music that was intentionally created to be perceived differently by its performers and listeners amounted to a small aesthetic revolution.

On the other hand, interruptions mean a complete cutoff of the musical phrase that lasts usually around 450 ms and 700 ms (timespans specific to compound modes). However, most times composers do not notate the precise duration of the interruptions, as it is an unwritten law that they should last as long as a complete transfer of attention (i.e. approximately 600 ms).

Professor Schama etc. specifically asked me to write in this chapter a couple of sentences dedicated to non-durations. Their importance in Temporalist musical practice is minimal, yet the old psychologist insisted that "although things generally seem to happen in the perceptual foreground, there is no foreground without a background. Therefore ignoring the latter's existence would be an act of temporal ignorance."

All that said, here is what I am supposed to put on paper: to the extent that the temporal continuum constitutes the background over which all discrete events captured by our perception occur, this backdrop does not simply disappear the moment the foreground of perception gets busy – for instance, with the musical pulsations of a Temporalist composition.

Herr Professor pointed out to me that even the most trained musicians of his world are not able to name – accurately and without guessing – the durations specific to the used temporal modes if these are materialized by only two pulsations: the first, whose duration is supposed to be recognized, and the second, marking the end of the first:

In order to define, our musical brain generally needs to compare at least two equal pulsations or, in the case of inertial temporal modes such as IOI 100 ms and IOI 150 ms, even more. Subjected to this test (i.e. recognizing temporal modes from the "partial fingerprint" of one duration), musicians were asked to continue themselves the mode that they, for better or for worse, had guessed. Everyone admitted to have done that by employing the mechanisms of estimative perception and apperception, that is, by comparing the presented duration with known musical contexts evoked by it. The conclusion of the experiment was that human acuity for single pulsations is impaired by the impossibility of ampler comparative/analytical cognitive processes – even in trained Temporalist musicians, who spent all their lives in an environment saturated with pulsations and their specific durations.

There also are in Temporalist music theory non-durations – timespans whose duration may be deduced rationally, but not perceived, not even by means of estimative perception. Examples abound and illustrate, as far as Temporalist psychologists are concerned, the insinuation of the above mentioned "background" through the interstices of the foreground, "like a clear sky through the luxuriant thicket of a tropical forest canopy". (Both I and Jean-Philippe were stunned upon hearing Herr Professor murmuring these words. Then, the mystery was dispelled by Miss Clara's catty stride.)

In Temporalist music there also is a kind of swing that, I was told, does not infringe upon the double cyclicity avoidance principle:

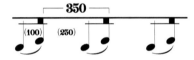

I asked how come this pulsatory structure goes uncensored since it is composed of at least three cycles: the "beat" (which is the most poignant) repeating itself every 350 ms; the anacrusical AR pulsations lasting each time 100 ms; and finally the crusical TH values, each lasting for 250 ms. Jean-Philippe, in spite of this evidence, told me that their swing contains only one temporal mode – IOI 350 ms, that is – established by the recurrence of the TH values. To my astonishment, Herr Professor nodded:

– Let's take them one at a time. The 100 ms long AR does not establish a temporal mode, as its duration is not confirmed, but refuted by the preceding TH value duration. We only know that it lasts for about 100 ms because it is perceptibly placed on the subjective rhythmization threshold. If it lasted, say, for 70 ms, it would be very close to the *crepitus* sensation, meaning that we would perceive it not as an anacrusis, but as a crushing note. On the other hand, if you didn't know, like I do, that it lasts for about 100 ms, and if you were consequently asked to repeat its duration in order to establish the temporal mode to which this AR pulsation belongs – you wouldn't be able to do it, due to our innate deficiency to reproduce and repeat accurately singular durations. Furthermore, there is no 350 ms long cyclicity from one AR pulsation to the next either, because if you were asked to create a superimposed IOI 350 ms mode made of these pulsations, you wouldn't be able to do it without elogizing the TH values as structural rests:

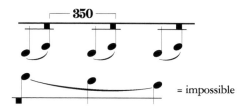

= impossible

Finally, the 250 ms long interval that separates any of the TH values from the following AR pulsation represents, perceptually, a non-duration, meaning a temporal segment that we are unable to experience, even by means of estimative perception. Furthermore, there is no way that we could create, by taking over this interval directly from the swing formula, a IOI 250 ms temporal mode that would possess prosodical capabilities. Well, this segment represents a modicum of the background that I told you about and that insinuated itself through the foreground pulsations. It often pervades the no man's land created in between two durationally unequal pulsations that establish a prosodical relationship of indetermination. You write this down in your book and forget about it – the important thing is that your readers know that these non-durations exist.

There was another context where this background popped up into our discussions. I will write about that in a chapter dedicated to larger than IOI 700 ms temporal modes.

Herr Schlezinger etc. asked me to introduce the IOI 700 ms temporal mode by briefly describing a phenomenon that our psychologists have called "the indifference interval". It seems that a series of experiments were conducted in which various isochronous sequences were presented to the subjects who in turn were asked to continue them by finger tapping. It was thus discovered that humans manifest a tendency to slacken down (positive deviation) isochronous pulsations situated in the IOI 100-700 ms range and speed up (negative deviation) those larger than IOI 700 ms. It was experimentally demonstrated that in between approximately IOI 600 ms and IOI 800 ms, people generally reproduce the presented sequences with inconclusive deviations. Most times the indifference interval was spotted close to the 700 ms value, and for this reason the corresponding temporal mode bears a peculiar significance. And yet, given the specific cultural background, Temporalist musicians relate differently to the premises of the above experiment. Within the IOI 100-400 ms range, the general tendency is for the presented isochronous sequences to be transformed into (or, rarely, deviated towards) the closest "temperate" mode. For instance, a Temporalist musician presented with a IOI 165 ms isochrony would generally continue it as a quicker IOI 150 ms, thus doing the opposite – in comparison to the subjects of our world. It is only in the IOI 450-600 ms range that the tendencies harmonize, along with the negative deviations in isochronous sequences larger that IOI 700 ms.

I assume that by now no one will be surprised if I say that the IOI 700 ms temporal mode is initially devised by Temporalist interpreters as the sum of two uneven pulsations: IOI 400 + IOI 300 ms. This trick may only be put at work by musicians who have already assimilated the IOI 400 ms mode. Beginners are allowed to imagine the "indifference mode" in a blatantly unorthodox manner, that is, linking two equal timespans: 350 ms + 350 ms.

The IOI 750 ms mode is conceived in a similar way, the two uneven divisions being 400 ms and 350 ms.

Although in Temporalist music schools the IOI 750 ms and IOI 800 ms compound modes are presented as isochronous sequences that must be learnt as such and assimilated by means of relative memorization, composers generally do not bother to notate them accordingly. Only didactic editions display nowadays the scholastic notation:

100

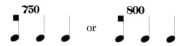

In commercial editions, which in principle respect composers' intentions, these compound modes are notated with structural rests marking the uneven divisions:

Most times interpreters are free to choose the way they want to imagine the sequence: 400 + 350 ms or 350 + 400 ms.

The IOI 800 ms compound mode is as "compound" as the IOI 400 ms mode was "primary". As an exception, theory books recommend that this mode be initially devised as 400 + 400 ms – and continued like any other normal isochronous sequence. Musicians, though, prefer to imagine it as 4 x 200 ms – which is against their tradition and very much to the gratuitous delight of my inner self as a great admirer of the durational hierarchizations specific to our bar-rhythmical system.

IOI 800 ms is also the first isochrony at whose pulsations' end we may spot the perceptual "background" that Professor Schüstermacher etc. had told me about. For this very reason, IOI 800 ms ends the series of compound temporal modes and marks the beginning of the estimative modes that encompass all isochronies from the IOI 850-2000 ms range.

The day dedicated to the presentation of larger-than-IOI 800 ms temporal modes started with an experiment that Herr Professor insisted would help me understand the three notions present in the title of this chapter. From the insides of a drawer, he produced a few sheets of paper already printed with squares and asked me to draw one myself, with or without a ruler – the important thing being that my square be perceptually identical to the printed one. I was not allowed to actually measure the original square any other way but visually. I did what I was asked to do and managed to draw a square that was quite similar to the original one. "Okeydokey", Herr Professor mumbled and, after a short while, added:

– This kind of immediate perception of equality is also put to work in the case of all isochronies from the IOI 100-800 ms range, even if in the IOI 450-800 ms segment the direct perception partially diminishes its intuitive nature due to the gradual diminishing of pulsatory inertia.

On the second sheet of paper there were printed three squares and as many dotted lines tilted at 15°, 30° and 45° respectively. The old psychologist asked me to reproduce the squares at the given inclinations. After doing that, he was not interested whether the dimensions of my squares were close to the original. He only asked me if I felt that it was becoming harder and harder to transpose graphically the geometrical equivalences. Indeed, the 45° tilted square was quite an ordeal to draw.

Herr Sch. etc.: The kind of "jamming" that was inflicted upon your perception by the fact that you had to incline the square is similar to that we experience whenever the isochronous durations are affected by the presence of a temporal gap – that is, projections of the perceptual background that we have recently discussed. The gap is actually a sensation that we perceive as a short interval of blank expectation. We start to experience it once with the IOI 850-1000 ms temporal modes and it becomes a dominant sensation for the IOI 1000-2000 ms range, progressively. The fact that we can still synchronize with the isochronous pulsations of these large temporal modes means that we mobilize the mechanisms of an estimative perception that gradually dwindles, starting to become seemingly inefficient for larger-than-IOI 2000 ms temporal modes.

The last sheet of paper was printed with a big square. Herr Professor asked me to look at it and do nothing at all – after which he called Clara, whom he told in German, while continuously pointing at his open mouth, that he was starving.

It was only during the lunch that Herr Schumpfel etc. served me with a blank sheet of paper and a pen, asking me to draw a square that would be identical in size with the one I was allowed to look at some fifteen minutes ago. Once again I did what I was told and, upon handling the paper back to the host, he crumpled it without even looking at my square.

Herr. Sch.: Well, this time you have *approximated* the size of the original square. It is possible that your approximation is quite accurate, but if you were to repeat the experiment, your squares will surely be either bigger or smaller than the original. Something similar takes place if you tried to synchronize to a temporal mode that is larger than IOI 2000 ms: you will notice that sometimes your tap coincides with the original pulsation. Some other times, you will tap quicker than you should – but most times you will be late.

Jean-Philippe, who was fighting with the edible sinews of an undecided animal, put aside the small saw he used to cut them into smaller pieces and brought us back from experimental psychology into the realm of music theory.

J.-P.: In musical *practice*, all temporal modes from the IOI 850-2000 ms range, and especially those larger than IOI 1000 ms, are attacked with help from a few interpretative tricks. If there are three instruments to be synchronised, a fourth player will "cheat" by building up the estimative mode with pulsations taken over from the known primary modes. For instance, if the sought after mode is IOI 1000 ms, the "cheater" will conduct the three instrumentalists by providing them with cues every 300+200+300+200 ms. After the first three so produced isochronous pulsations, the conductor stops and lets the instrumentalists continue the IOI 1000 ms temporal mode by themselves. Yet, let us not forget that apart from a group of composers who, a few generations ago, had a sudden crush for the lascivious estimative modes, these were and are largely underused in our musical tradition. I suggest that we bother no more with them and celebrate the fact that soon our guest will have learnt the theoretical ABC of our music!

I managed to go outside for an hour, as planned. I enjoyed revisiting our *arrondissement* after more than two years (although its walls were covered with the same posters). I tried to assess my writing so far and was appalled remembering that my guides asked me to describe Temporalist music in less than two hundred pages. "People should just get a basic idea", Jean-Philippe used to say. "Your book should be no more, no less than «food for thought»", added Herr Professor. The problem is that, in a very short time, I have completed the first hundred pages and was unable to present at least the ABC of their musical theory. Nothing yet about the pulsatory passages! Or should I call them "temporal modulations"? Again, almost nothing about crushing notes or about the "dotted" pulsatory structures. I still do not know whether I will find room in the book for concepts such as "integrality" or non-modal AR values. What on Earth would my readers understand about "pulsatory contextualization" without having listened to at least a Temporalist *bagatelle*? And... *mon Dieu!*, when and where shall I describe the art of pulsatory groupings, a subject of which my own knowledge is so limited? And – should I dedicate a chapter to the many months I have spent observing the way their students learn music? Jean-Philippe insisted that I offer many details about this particular experience, so that their theory would not look like a mere abstraction.

I know what I should do: I shall put down on paper everything that I consider worth being written – after which I will let the manuscript "age" for several months and, during this the summer, I shall start eliminating pages.

Back home, I found on the kitchen counter this note from my wife:

My little stud,
I am away, not knowing when I'll be able to return. You can manage with the food, right? Apart from that, when you reached the middle-age crisis, some fifteen years ago, we did a lot of talking and we both managed to get through it. I now understand that you slowly approach your 60th birthday and have thoughts about death and about the fact that after a while nobody will remember you. I assume this is why you started writing. I support you in that and wish you luck. Please just don't swallow any more Viagra pills without consulting a doctor first. The last nights were comical, but you don't have to prove me anything. That mistress of yours – when is she returning from America?
S.

I must call the pharmacy and tell them that I'm taking the whole week off. In just a few days I managed to make my wife believe that I am impotent and frustrated – while in reality I feel like flying from one flower to another, like a happy bumblebee.

With the exception of directional accents, in temporal modes defined by the *crepitus* sensation, there are no thesis values. The "melodic climax accents" are marked for the consciousness even in the absence of any prosodical structures (i.e. anacrusical or metacrusical). The only such relationship that may occur here is that of "crushing note(s)" established between an AR pulsation (or a group of AR pulsations) and the directional TH. There are no TH-AR interpulsatory relationships in the area defined by the *crepitus* sensation. Herr Schlattner etc. presented to me all these perceptual phenomena so that I would better understand why a TH pulsation, followed by a metacrusical AR, in order to be perceived as such, cannot last for less than about 100 ms – which in turn explains why the subjective rhythmization threshold is placed precisely in this area, the first where we may speak with confidence about metacrusical relationships between pulsations.

As concerns the construction of some anacrusical, *inegalité* structures, this only becomes a possibility if the TH values recur every 220 ms – the duration of the accent being about 120 ms and that of the non-accent about 100 ms. Within the 50 ms grid, the first *inegalité* structure is possible starting with a TH value recurrence at every 250 ms (which, I was told, does not imply that the TH value lasts for exactly 150 ms and the AR for a sharp 100 ms).

Henceforth there is a whole debate about how "tempered" modern Temporalist music is in fact, because while isochronous rows remain stuck with the 50 ms grid, pulsations may become quite lax durationally if implied in the construction of such non-isochronous, recurring structures. It seems that the general rule is that at least the attack of TH values fit within the 50 ms grid – the *inegalité* just described being such an example: the TH values will reiterate precisely every 250 ms while lasting, my guides informed me, for about 135 ms. The psychophysical phenomena that lay behind such pulsatory structures are irrelevant for musical practice, which used such off-grid durations long before they were recognized as such, the same way the first American jazz guitarists used intuitively those blue notes situated outside the tempered dodecaphonic system.

A second debate refers to the non-isochronous (or uneven) temporal modes – the "dotted rhythms" or the swing from our musical terminology being a handy example. These are known by Temporalists as *double modes* (or *uneven double modes*), as they are composed by the recurrence of two pulsations having different durational and prosodical values. In the case of double modes whose pulsations strictly submit to the 50 ms grid, their names are given by the constituent durations – for example, IOI 200+250:

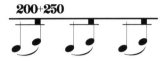

On the other hand, when the 50 ms grid is only confirmed by the placement of the TH values, the non-isochronous mode is named after the durational interval established by two consecutive TH values – for example, TH 250 ms.

Temporalist music theory schoolbooks (which are mainly based on the stylistic precepts belonging to a time period that was as mannerist as our Viennese Classicism) claim that the TH 250 ms temporal mode proves the fact that a prosodical TH value, in order to be perceived as such, may last for less than 120 ms only in the case of the IOI 100 ms isochronous mode (isochronous modes with a ternary profile are excluded from this debate). For double modes, the minimum duration of a prosodical TH is about 120 ms. During the mentioned time period, although the 50 ms grid was already established as a standard, the old modes and their specific durations (120 ms in our case) were still granted the status of "natural" versions. (I wonder how many of our musicians are able to recognize instantly a natural major third…).

Given the fact that in the TH 250 ms double mode the TH pulsations were observed to last about 135 ms, the theory seems to be confirmed and Temporalists composers use it quite often, mostly in its AR+TH, swing-like version.

J.-P.: In the inverted succession that you call Lombard rhythm…

Me: I have never come across this term.

J.-P.: Lombard *inegalité*?

Me: No…

Herr. Sch. etc.: *Scotch snap* from the *Scottish strathspey*?

Me: I think that you really should have imported a real musician. In 1012, it will have been fifty years since I took my first piano lessons, but I have never heard, in my entire life, of this Scotch brand!

J.-P.: The fifth *Étude*, in E minor, opus 25? Chopin?

Finally, they were talking in my language. *That* Chopin *Étude* about which two of my piano teachers advised me *not* to split the beats in four equal parts in order to find out the length of the sixteenth notes.

Now Jean-Philippe was telling me the same thing, this time in Temporalist terminology: the TH value will last for about 100-120 ms, marking the subjective rhythmization threshold. In the case of a theoretical TH 250 ms (TH+AR) Lombard rhythm, the pulsatory inertia and the shortness of the TH value make the double mode unsustainable:

For this reason, in Temporalist music, the first sustainable TH+AR double mode is considered to be TH 300 ms. If the metronome indication from my edition of Chopin Studies was notated by the composer himself, it means that my guides were right: between TH 300 ms (TH+AR) and TH 326 ms (TH+AR) there lays precisely the small difference that Chopin wanted to communicate when he wrote at the beginning of the *Étude* the word *leggiero*.

Hanging on the walls of many of the Temporalist music schools, there was an inscription of whose signification I was eventually made curious, so I asked Jean-Philippe to tell me what was their musical *Liberté, égalité, fraternité* – or maybe their version of the Leninist slogan that my uncle Gérard, an ever smiling *gauchiste* and a plain imbecile, used to tell me when I was a little child and after having observed how passionate I was about my piano playing: "Practice, practice and again – practice!!!" Surprisingly, the number one slogan of Temporalist music schools did not belong to a politician, but to a pedagogue who died some 150 years ago, ("a kind of Temporalist Czerny", as he was presented to me): "Nothing is impossible beyond xxx!", "xxx" being the real and untranslatable name of the IOI 100 ms temporal mode. The slogan, Jean-Philippe told me, still awaits to be confirmed – and it did not transform the Lombard TH 250 ms double mode in a sustainable repetitive structure.

One of the most musically relevant psychophysical laws stipulates that, within the temporal interval specific to the minimum acton (about 180-200 ms), there cannot exist, at the level of human perception, more than one accent. Two accents may share this time span only if they belong to two different actons (pulsatory structures):

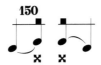

This law explains why the fast subjective rhythmization threshold coincides with IOI 100 ms and why this threshold is different for ternary structures (i.e. around IOI 70 ms) – every second (third, respectively) pulsation, a new TH may be placed/perceived.

The fact that in the IOI 100 ms temporal mode a second TH value may be placed at the *limit* of the minimum acton specific interval makes it be perceived as a secondary accent:

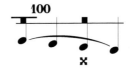

Yet, in Temporalist scores, nobody notates it as a TH value, but as an AR:

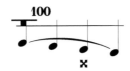

108

Rarely, the secondary accent *is* notated, for IOI 150 ms...

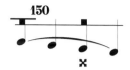

...but, more likely, the above structure is notated like this:

Before burying myself in the grand university libraries of the Temporalist world I had been scheduled to follow a brief course of Temporalist musical orthography. However, Jean-Philippe cancelled that, saying that since Herr Professor imposed on me the use of the zeuxilogic semiography, I should invent for myself the notational rules that would represent prosodical structures or hint at the involved psychophysical phenomena etc. As "zeuxilogic semiography" is rather an aspirational concept imagined and promoted by Herr Professor and passed over to me, I do not see why I should bother now to give it a polished shape. I will use the notation illustratively while making the promise that, if the Hell freezes over and this book will sell more than 500 copies, for a second edition I will make the effort to create a chapter dedicated to the above mentioned musical orthography. It will be quite an ordeal, though, to transpose all graphical elements that I have noticed in the Temporalist notation into this "open" zeuxilogic semiography.

The concept of "secondary accent" is still present in IOI 200 and 250 ms temporal modes, but I rarely saw these accents notated as such in Temporalist scores:

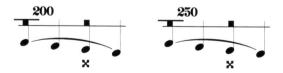

In academic Temporalist theory, secondary accents cease to exist starting with IOI 300 ms. It is considered that from the first TH to the next a complete transfer of attention is being consumed (about 600 ms) and, as a matter of consequence, the second accent cannot be considered as secondary. To my perception, which is 100% educated within the bar-rhythmical system, the second TH remains secondary, as it is not backed up by the metric accent, as the case is with the first TH:

During the many months spent listening to piles of recorded Temporalist music and following the corresponding scores with my eyes, I have noticed that for temporal modes from the IOI 400-550 ms range interpreters pay more attention to the sonorous marking of the prosodical relationships. As, in this area, the attention shift from one pulsation to the next is sustainable, and as in the absence of a bar-rhythmical skeleton, the placement of the TH and AR pulsations is not always easily fathomable, performers either use more sounds for the TH values (if their instruments allow that)…

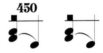

…place intensity accents (stress) on every TH value, or become more attentive with the melodic line, given the fact that all Temporalists, musicians or not, associate descending notes with metacrusical relationships and ascending notes with anacrusical ones, repeated notes indicating different relationships of prosodical indetermination:

Finally, some instrumentalists mark the prosody by alternating *legato* and *staccato* note attacks. This interpretative trick becomes a rule in the case of compound isochronous modes from the IOI 600-800 ms range. Here, the last pulsation of a prosodical structure is either attacked *staccato*, or its sonorous materialization is suppressed somewhere in the middle:

110

Temporal modes from the IOI 850-2000 ms range are so rarely used as isochronous rows that I used to wonder why separate chapters are dedicated to them in Temporalist schoolbooks. Most times their composers use these modes to keep the timbral (and not so much the pulsatory) contribution of an instrument alive. Anyway, due to the sensible presence of the pulsatory gap, prosodical relationships between successive notes in these large modes require a supplementary mental effort, so that pulsations be imagined as part of the same temporal window. Beyond IOI 2000 ms, Temporalists consider that prosodical relationships cease to have any musical significance.

Although I had plenty of opportunities to fall in love with Temporalist music theory, I don't know why that happened only when my guides presented to me the crushing notes. Before that lesson, as a piano player, I used to associate *acciaccatura* with the idea of "as fast as possible in the given context" and with those smaller musical notes that are most times cut with an oblique stroke. Jean-Philippe told me that, when he first discovered in our scores the acciaccatura, he felt that between the two musico-temporal universes there is after all a bridge, given the fact that, in our music theory too, *acciaccatura* is associated with non-accentuation and it is the only rhythmical symbol that is linked to a particular perceptual threshold – that responsible for the *crepitus* sensation.

When I found out what the subject of our next lesson was, I asked something like "And what is there to be learned about an ordinary *acciaccatura?*".

J.-P.: For instance, *acciaccatura* may help you tell apart the IOI 100 ms and the IOI 150 ms temporal modes. The latter is the first isochrony whose pulsations may be preceded by *acciaccaturas*. In the former's case, *acciaccaturas* are not possible, no matter the context.

The rationale behind that is simple. Given that an *acciaccatura* lasts for about 50 ms, in the case of IOI 100 ms, it would occupy half the length of the actual pulsation, thus creating a hypothetical IOI 50 ms mode, a *"crepitus* mode" placed beyond the possibility of subjective rhythmization. Not to mention that the *acciaccatura* and the actual pulsation could not, under these circumstances, hierarchize accordingly. It was easier for me to understand this psychophysical phenomenon when Jean-Philippe invited me to sit on the bench of the rückpositiv. He was already improvising note passages in the IOI 100 ms mode when he asked me to do the same two octaves below – trying in the same time to crush with *acciaccaturas* some of the pulsations. Indeed, I felt that it was impossible. IOI 150 ms contains just the necessary respite of about 50 ms for pulsations to be both crushed with *acciaccaturas* and remain in the area of subjective rhythmization. Jean-Philippe asked me to test myself this temporal mode, and place *acciaccaturas* here and there – which I found easily doable.

Before the implementation of the 50 ms grid, musicians used two types of *acciaccaturas*: the "strong" *acciaccatura* and the "weak" *acciaccatura*. The first one, lasting for about 50 ms, survived to this day, while the weak one, lasting for about 70 ms, became optional and may be used in all temporal modes starting from IOI 200 ms. After being asked to feel the difference between the two kinds of *acciaccatura*, my guides told me that the weak *acciaccatura* differentiates very well the IOI 150 ms and the IOI 200 ms temporal modes, as the former cannot "tolerate" it, because it would push the crushed pulsations under the subjective rhythmization threshold: 150 ms – 70 ms = 80 ms.

Herr Schickele etc. asked me to use the following zeuxilogic notation for *acciaccaturas*:

I was made attentive that not every *acciaccatura* note lasts for about 50 ms (or 70 ms). These values are specific to a so called "*acciaccatura* space" that may be materialized by means of a single pulsation or more – four at most, given that the fifth should be the crushed note, as we only have five fingers on one hand. Such *acciaccaturas* were given proper names in Temporalist music theory, so we can speak of double, triple or quadruple *acciaccaturas*. Professor Schippenward etc., whose scholarly verve started to amuse me, asked me to remember a detail that is musically irrelevant, but nonetheless interesting. Some double *acciaccaturas* and all the trilpe and quadruple ones reach what our psychologists call "the temporal order threshold". Our host explained to me that, if *acciaccaturas* had not possessed melodic unidirectionality and if they could instead be materialized by means of intervallic leaps, our perception would make us witness an interesting paradox:

If the *acciaccatura* pulsations last for less than 30 ms each, our brain will discern the fact that they are not synchronous, but will not help us tell which their actual order is. That does not imply that in the case of unidirectional *acciaccaturas* it would help but, at least for Temporalists, the fact that at the level of their apperceptive expectations multiple *acciaccaturas* are associated with melodic unidirectionality makes them process correctly, at a cognitive level, the order of pulsations.

I asked my two guides whether, given the fact that *acciaccatura* pulsations cannot be more than four in a row, we could speak of a specific temporal mode, with variants – the same way IOI 300 ms and

IOI 350 ms are considered to be a dual representation of a single pulsatory functionality. I was told that acc*iaccatura pul*sations are more like a kind of "filling" of the *acciaccatura* space, because we cannot control in any way the isochronicity of these pulsations. Trying to be more illustrative, Herr Professor drew a strange human hand, with a very long pinky and gradually shorter fingers:

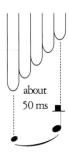

Herr Sch. etc.: Such a pianist's hand, which can produce a sound with the shortest finger only before all the other four fingers have touched the keys of the instrument, will help you understand what kind of *acciaccatura* space filling I was talking about. If between the longest finger and the shortest one there is a 50 ms long time interval, the interpulsatory relationship that will be produced belongs to the *crepitus* category, and not to the anacrusical type, that can only be established once the subjective rhythmization threshold is reached. The fact that between the first *acciaccatura* pulsation and the crushed note there may be interference from one to three more pulsations does not alter in any way the *crepitus* functional relationship. In order to stress the fact that *acciaccaturas* are placed beyond the rhythmization threshold, our string players usually materialize them as *glissandi:*

During the months spent in Temporalist musical libraries, I had the time to notice that *acciaccaturas* do not play a structural role in written Temporalist music. Most times composers use them as "markings for consciousness", to stress the TH value of certain pulsations that, unless crushed, could trigger some undesired prosodical ambiguities.

Despite the fact that, at some point I held in my hands a contemporary score in which *crepitus* pulsations were *not* used as *acciaccaturas* (that is, confined to the 50-70 ms time interval), but as a kind of temporal modes:

Upon looking at the score, Jean-Philippe shrugged and told me that it is either the music of a negligent or uncultivated composer, or some pulsations meant to go beyond the rhythmization threshold, towards the attainable (with the right instrument) IOI 70 ms, or an improvisatory passage.

– What? Since when do you improvise? I goggled, after almost two years in which I only observed a pious respect for the written pulsation.

Jean-Philippe smiled mysteriously and replied rabbinically:

– Sometimes we get sleepy too…

115

My first piano teacher (in total they were nine, if I do not include my mother) is the only one of whom I kept a disagreeable memory. Not because he chain smoked, puffing the choking clouds directly into my mouth, but because he addressed me with the expression "my little Polish boy", not knowing that the name Pogoriloffsky comes from a white Russian ancestor who fell in love with my paternal grandmother (a war widow), consequently marrying her and adopting her two children at the beginning of the 1920s. Well, this professor called Jaschinsky, a Pole from Soviet Ukraine, kept reminding me at the beginning of each lesson that "music is exclusively made of scales, arpeggios and leaps". In the first months of my musical education I was consequently forced to perform scales in all tonalities, one hour a day. That was the only period in my life when I hated the piano. This is why I involuntarily flinched the moment Herr Schwarowsky etc. informed me that "music is composed of temporal modes, passages and pulsatory groupings".

After having assimilated the seven primary modes, the young Temporalist musicians are tortured for a while with the passages from one temporal mode to another. In order to understand the concept, Jean-Philippe asked me to think of these passages as if they were some kind of pulsatory modulations, in which the important thing ceases to be the two modes, but the affect triggered by the passage itself.

J.-P.: Any student who has just assimilated the primary modes is able to make the translation from one such IOI to another – but only if the number of pulsations is indefinite. If things remained in this stage, the passages from one mode to another would only occur by placing the last pulsation (or the last pulsations) of the initial IOI in one temporal window (A) and by placing the first pulsation (or the first pulsations) of the second IOI in another temporal window (B):

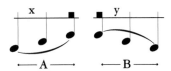

If you want, these kinds of passages look like the sudden, chromatic modulations that I learnt of from your Harmony Treatises. In the example I have just presented to you, the interval between the two TH values,

116

although lasting like all the preceding x pulsations, is a non-duration both because it is placed in between two indeterminant pulsations and in between two temporal windows. For this reason, the affect triggered by the passage is lost into the perceptual background that our host described to you a few days ago.

The interpretative difficulties start when the last pulsation (or the last pulsations) of the initial mode and the first pulsation (or the first pulsations) of the next mode create prosodical relationships, while some or all pulsations creating such a structure belong to the same temporal window:

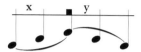

In this example, Jean-Philippe assured me, the TH pulsation belongs to the x mode, although its duration is specific to the y mode. The passage from the first mode to the second takes place somewhere between the TH value and the first metacrusical AR. That – I was asked to accept in the absence of a direct personal experience – generates to the interpreter of the pulsatory structure a particular affect that must be kept in the inventory of his or her affective memory in order to be used later, when the respective musician will have to decode interpretatively the most intricate pulsatory groupings that Temporalist composers were able to devise.

J.-P.: If you want, the last example may be compared to a diatonic modulation, as the TH from the initial anacrusical formula becomes the metacrusical TH in the second part of the pulsatory structure: one pulsation serving two functionalities, the same way a major chord may be in the same time the subdominant of an initial tonality and the tonic of the tonality to which the modulation goes.

There are many ways to imagine pulsatory passages within a single temporal window. Here are just a few examples:

A third type of passage, that gets students closer to the art of pulsatory groupings, is made by means of a pulsation whose duration differs both from the span of the initial IOI and from that of the IOI to which the passage goes:

The set of rules by which these passages are admitted in the system of academic norms fill dozens of pages in Temporalist Temporal Harmony tomes. I was advised not to try to learn them, since not having the chance of becoming a practitioner of Temporalist music I could not have even a minimal representation of the psycho-temporal realities that ultimately led to the formulation of the respective rules. In order to overcome this inherent handicap, Jean-Philippe helped me represent this new musical world by making a surprising comparison…

In the long hours in which we both pulled the gig that was parked at some point in Herr Schamazing's etc. paved front yard, we discovered that we both were ardent supporters of the Olympique Lyonnais football team, although we never lived in the city that hosts it. You cannot imagine what a strange couple we made: two men, looking like any other Temporalists in their fifties, discussing enthusiastically, in French, about *Les Gones*, strategies, goals and victories.

All these being said, here is how, months after that, Jean-Philippe explained to me the way a Temporalist music "player" gets professional. At first you have to learn how to place yourself so as to realize the position where the ball that was just passed on to you is going to fall. Once you reach it, in principle you must be able to stop it, place it into an optimal kick position, decide to which player from you team you should pass it to – and kick it precisely to the desired spot. Jean-Philippe called all these steps "the training context" in which all you have to do is to follow the mentioned steps without failure and without any extra steps. Roughly, this is the professional context of a young student who has just assimilated the primary temporal modes and is able to perform various passages from one isochronous mode to another, either one belonging to a distinct temporal window.

In the next stage, the football player is supposed to compress the above stages in a single "whole", so that the moment he reaches the ball he knows how to kick it, without stopping it first, in the direction of the right teammate. This is the special talent of "game situation assessment" that sport commentators speak of. *Mutatis mutandis*, Temporalist music virtuosi must be able to go from one IOI to the next even if the pulsations these are composed of are not enough to transform them into some proper temporal modes.

This is the point where Herr Schummeniger etc. intervened, telling us, very much amused, that while he lived in the United Kingdom, he had the opportunity to read the study of a psychologist who had decomposed all the stages that the psycho-motor complex of a tennis player has to follow when he or she must guess the trajectory, velocity and the bounce angle of the ball in order to coordinate these with the steps, the arm movements, the intensity of the hit, the angle of attack and the target area in the opponent's field. The author intentionally left no imaginable stage unaccounted for and corroborated everything with countless academic references, quoting especially authors that were granted access to the ISI publications. The conclusion of the study? A professional tennis player cannot play this sport at an average speed of the ball (at the moment of the kick) of 190-200 kilometers per hour, because that is scientifically impossible. The fact that reality invalidates the psychophysics terribly amused our host. The study also quoted an ATP top performer who said that many times when he hits the ball with the racket he feels like the action has already taken place in a very near past.

My guides made all this athletic detour so that I understand the importance of assimilating the individual affective states provoked by various kinds of passages from one IOI to another. If these were impossible to be stored into the "temporal memory" – a concept that is heavily circulated in the Temporalist musical world –, the interpreters of the complicated pulsatory groupings would have followed the steps of the tennis player who, from a scientific point of view, is unable to return the ball into the opponent's field.

In this example, which is very much exaggerated for the sake of the demonstration, there are present no less than seven pulsations and four IOIs.

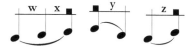

No Temporalist interpreter would decompose this pulsatory structure into temporal modes in order to extract the specific duration for each pulsation. First, there is no sufficient time for all these cognitive processes, especially given the circumstances that in Temporalist musical practice the alternative of studying difficult musical segments in a slower tempo is not possible.

The only way to achieve this particular ability, which has no correspondence in our musical world, is musicians' step by step assimilation of the way every type of IOI to IOI passage resonates affectively. Thus, after the years in which the main focus is assimilating the temporal modes, students start wrestling with a new concept called "contextualization". Before entering a music university, students are supposed to be able to pass from one IOI to another in every imaginable prosodical context ever devised by Temporalist composers. There are hundreds, maybe thousands of Studies composed by pedagogy specialists to help young Temporalists get through this difficult stage of their education. Thus, the limit of the "training context" is reached, after which there are gradually introduced groups of only two pulsations belonging to the same IOI. In these advanced Studies, passages from one IOI to the next become tighter and tighter, and the students who did not work hard enough during the previous training stage will encounter great difficulties in deciphering interpretatively these intricate pulsatory structures. Those who still rely on their relational memory and have not yet reached an absolute memory for the affects triggered by the various passages from one IOI to another will not get through this stage in their musical training too soon.

A century ago, this is where the ABC of the future Temporalist interpreters would make a definitive halt. Back then, no composer dared to place in one temporal window three or more pulsations having different durations.

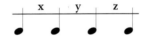

It was meant for Temporalist music too to encounter a „Schönberg" who, even if he did not serialize the seven primary modes, had the gift of composing a few dozen works dedicated to that "keratin baleen" instrument in which IOIs would change at an amazing rate – for the ears of his audiences. As his detractors dubbed him a mere *Papiermusik* composer, he toured the cities performing his works himself, with a temporal accuracy that allowed no room for any more ill intended grumbles.

Soon, his bizarre mannerism became fashionable – and today you cannot get the equivalent of a Master's Degree without demonstrating that you are capable of producing interpretatively any combination of pulsations taken from the inventory of the primary modes.

J.-P.: Our "football players" develop the capacity to concentrate in one Gestalt-type move the stop, the positioning and the well placed kick of the ball. You probably know that parable: if you ask a millipede how he manages to coordinate his many legs, he will stumble right away. The parable is well suited for our musicians. The elaborated pulsatory structures they currently perform are not analyzed at all when produced, but read directly the same way we read French written words, photographically. Yet, this reading cannot be made in the absence of a sizeable apperceptive background, created during the thousands of hours spent by our musicians in the realm of interpulsatory contextualizations.

(Summer of 2008)
I have just read this chapter and I wonder if someone who has never listened to Temporalist music will ever understand a word of my description, given the fact that pulsatory passages and their affective fingerprint become pure abstraction in the absence of the very music that uses them as construction materials.

I remember Jean-Philippe's effort to make me understand the right meaning of "affectivity", as the original Temporalist word has no corresponding term in the French language. The concept may be formulated as "affects that are discernible within a certain context". As usual, my friend produced a comparison that I omitted to mention when I wrote this chapter. Jean-Philippe rushed to the rückpositiv and started to improvise some choral-like harmonic progressions:

C — F — G — C

Cm — Fm — G — C

C — D7 — G — C

J.-P.: All three progressions end with a "passage" from G major to C major. From a physical point of view, the last two chords in the three examples are identical. The harmonic context they are placed into, though, differs significantly from one progression to another and, for this reason, an educated ear will discern the functional dissimilarities of the two chords at an "affective" level: authentic cadence in C major, Picardy cadence in C minor and interrupted cadence in G major, respectively. The way it is possible to move from one chord to another in many harmonic contexts, the same way we can move from one temporal mode to another or from an IOI to another. The problem that emerges in our musical practice is that many times these contextualized passages take place at a pace that does not leave room for analysis and therefore they are merged by our interpreters in Gestalt-like structures that only bear musical meaning as a whole.

As in fact the subject is way over my head, it is perhaps a better idea that I describe my own experience with pulsatory structures from this category. Before leaving me alone for the first time to listen to recorded music in a Temporalist musical library, Jean-Philippe recommended that, whenever I would spot repetitions in the scores, I try tapping the respective pulsations myself.

J.-P.: We won't be able to transform you into a Temporalist musician, but a closer contact with the music that you listen to will familiarize you better with our musical tradition. I was myself very much helped, years ago, by the fact that I hummed the repetitive passages from your music, even if it was a melodic line from an Alban Berg opera. Make a habit of tapping all the pulsatory structures whose discrete profile you think you can anticipate.

Jean-Philippe's advice was a good one. It was this way that I managed to assimilate the primary temporal modes that I often times used to tap on the libraries' tables. In addition, I started to understand the nature of Temporalist musical performance. I would notice in the score that a difficult section was about to be performed again and I could swear that I would be able to tap it myself… only to see once again how the pulsations pass by my brain and fingers, which could only hit the table awkwardly. "How on Earth do they do it?!" I asked myself aloud.

(Summer of 2008)

I have just remembered that in Temporalist musical high schools almost every classroom is provided with an instrument that only produces some clicks, and that is made of two short keyboards (10 keys each) placed one on top of the other. Whoever uses the top keyboard will notice that the lower one moves in synchrony. Not the other way round, though. "Double clickers" are used by music teachers to familiarize students with the temporal profile of some intricate structures that the young musicians are not yet able to disentangle interpretatively themselves. The student would let his ten fingers rest relaxed over the lower keys, while the teacher makes him or her feel and hear the pulsatory succession by handling the upper keyboard. The method, I was explained, is not considered to be very musical and for that reason many teachers do not agree with it. It becomes very useful, though, for students who feel that they have reached a dead end and to whom any way out would be salutary.

Jean-Philippe assured me that pulsatory contextualization is a musician's task that lasts a lifetime. Composers from the last three generations used to improvise or invent various structures, evaluate them aesthetically and only after that ask themselves if they can put them on paper, so that an interpreter would know how to produce them according to the composer's initial intentions. Jean-Philippe's grandfather, an intimate of those creators who exchanged such ideas some 90 years ago, told to his grandson that, in those times, they would gather periodically in the home of one of the composers to do just that: present new works or excerpts from the yet unwritten music. The most enigmatic structures were minutely debated and eventually notated, after a common effort of graphical representation. If the score was published, the musicians were eager to disseminate amongst instrumentalists the correct manner in which this or that difficult pulsatory structure was supposed to be tackled. Those who later followed exclusively this creative pathway became exclusivist composers who only wrote solo pieces, because they considered music to be a dialogue with *one's own* brain and a continuous challenge of *one own's* pulsatory-temporal competence. Perhaps I should dedicate a separate chapter to these folks too.

One day I had just left the library of a grand university and was heading to the lush strip of land that bordered the School of Agriculture. I used to enjoy there the brisk autumnal air and the contents of the food package whose existence and consistence was taken care of, each morning, by my dear friend Jean-Philippe. This time, though, my "secret" nook was occupied by a *clochard* who seemed to be waiting for me, if I were to consider just the welcoming gestures he kept doing. His presence was even stranger as I was told that, despite the generally modest standard of living, in their world such pauperism had been long abolished. The man was probably in his early forties, although he looked tired and ruffled like a Stahanovist working two shifts in a row at the lampblack factory. Although several months had passed since I started to get accustomed to translating the mental representation of the words Temporalists would address to me in their idiom, the verbal torrent the bum flooded me with was too dense for my "optimized" brain. I only remember that several concepts kept appearing in my consciousness: "mistake", "grand", "distraction", "music" and "truth". After finishing his oral dissertation – of which I did not understand a word – the *clochard* bent over the tree stub that I used to sit on during my lunch breaks, picked up from there a kind of backpack that was surprisingly clean, neat and fashionable and, from its insides, produced a halved clicker that he placed in one expert move on the stub – and started to exemplify, for my immediate enlightenment, several pulsatory structures of which, again, I could not manage to make any sense. Perhaps if the instrument produced some pitches I might have been tempted to understand what he was trying so hard to demonstrate. After ten minutes or so, the *clochard* stopped, thanked me (I still wonder what for) and stomped with long strides out onto the alley that led to the campus exit.

That evening I was anxious to meet Jean-Philippe and ask him whether he had any idea who that character might have been. Upon hearing my description, my friend started to laugh, as he identified the head of the Philosophy Department, a well known specialist in a discipline that may be translated as "speculative pulsatology". He was, I found out, a full fledged musician and psychologist, but at some point in his career he directed his preoccupations towards the most abstract academic and para-academic Temporalist disciplines. The school of thought the "*clochard*" embraced was based, roughly, on two ideas:

- any kind of pulsatory structure that may be defined conceptually – defines in its turn a segment of pulsatology (as a whole);

124

- pitches and the exclusive use of a certain set of temporal modes represent a mere convention or an aesthetic compromise that limits the universe of possibilities in which humans may relate themselves to discrete time.

For this reason, music can be but subservient to some imposed limitations that only give birth to aesthetic trends and stylistic paradigms, whereas speculative pulsatology is enhanced with every newly discovered "particular case". For instance, in these philosophers' view, the bar-rhythmical system, with all its augmentations, diminutions and multiple hierarchizations, cohabits quite well with the Temporalist modes, as we already know them. That is because, our *clochard* and his kind believe, both systems are mere "particular cases".

– And yet, what do they actually do for a living? I asked Jean-Philippe.

– Their preoccupation is the discovery and the cultivation of "the Possible", the musician replied. These scholars simply want to see how much our discrete/continuous temporal competence may spread, and that is why they invent or discover various pulsatory structures that look more like some equations. If you want, they represent the radicalized wing of our "Schönberg". They are not interested in the aesthetic dimension of the "equations" they produce – only in the extent to which these enlarge or not, within their domain of interest, the universe of possibility. Between "them" and "us", if I am permitted that demarcation, there is another category of pulsatologists who use or create such "equations" to enhance *their own* temporal experience and competence. That is indeed a world apart, made of artists who compose short and intricate pulsatory structures, dedicated to a special audience. If you want, their art is something like cryptic poetry – as opposed to the "epic poems" of the music that you may listen to in our concert halls. Pulsatory poems are published as scores, and those who like this kind of creations decipher them at home for their own intellectual enjoyment consisting of both aesthetic delight, cerebral masochism and the joy of knowledge. I can tell you that there were quite a few great "poets" of this kind, not to mention that I am myself an admirer of this sort of creativity – to which unfortunately you will never be granted access, as in this case we do not seek to listen to something. It is all about what the reader of the poem feels, thinks and understands.

The next day, Jean-Philippe actually produced a few pulsatory poems. From a graphical point of view, I must confess that they looked quite impressive, though their meaning was alien to me. My friend explained to me that the first one contained no less than three systems of discrete time representation that were juxtaposed in a dialogical manner. Apart from the primary modes that I immediately spotted, the score contained – well, yes! – rhythmical values al well (I assume those created some bizarre IOIs for a Temporalist ear). In addition, the primary modes were garnished with some intermediary IOIs that were not defined by means of some precise durational values, but with help from some symbols indicating that a certain mode was supposed to be performed "a little bit" faster or slower than usual.

The second poem displayed an incredible concentration of thesis values that made it unreadable as it was. Jean-Philippe explained to me that the "solution" of the puzzle was the transformation of certain TH values into AR pulsations. The pulsatory equation was conceived in such a way so that one transformation triggered another, while the third could return the first transformed pulsation to its initial TH value. An enigma-poem with one possible solution that a competent reader might find after a few hours of trial and errors, intuitions and labyrinthine intellectual ramblings.

Finally, the third poem probed the territory (copiously avoided by Temporalist musicians) of pulsations in *accelerando* and *decelerando*.

The sheer imagination of these creators filled Jean-Philippe with admiration. Yet, as the true lovers of this peculiar art form a very small community, it is no wonder that Temporalist resources are rarely, if ever, directed to its support. That, my guide added, does not explain why the philosopher I met by the tree stub forgets to change his clothes at least once a week.

After making an idea about the speculative amplitude Temporalist civilization managed to get to in matters regarding discrete time (and not only), I asked Jean-Philippe to provide me with a short yet powerful argument that would help me convince musicians of my world that the theoretical principles I epitomize in this book deserve their attention. My friend told me that he would think about that and tell me if he found an argument. More than six months passed since that talk and it just happened that our pathways once again crossed with the ever touring Madame Temporalissima's (and her cloned piano). The lady – a natural calamity as a person and a portrait of the stereotypes our musicians associate with viola playing tenors – was able to distinguish the sounds of the French language, but could only express her thoughts in the Temporalist idiom and (here I am supposed to insert a prolonged ellipsis) Finnish.

My Temporalist friends will pardon me for inserting in "their" book a few pages to explain the reasons why, whenever I hear the words "Finland" or "Finnish", I react allergically, with a strange and mildly painful contraction of my nipples…

I was finish… ing my third term at Sorbonne when my father asked me whether I would be tempted to apply for a programme that used to send students to various summer courses. "You know, that kind of academic spree where geeks only think of having sex with people that they will never see again", he told me. I think I replied with half of an answer, but that was sufficient to send me, five months after that discussion, to the bus platform of a small university-town. In Helsinki, where the plane landed, I managed to call the university secretariat and it was explained to me that there are street signs "everywhere" that point towards the campus. Between the last cigarette I smoked at Orly and the one I was about to light there was a nine hour smokeless intermission that I was eager to cut short, but my cigarette lighter had been silently confiscated by a bald Italian with dirty fingernails. It was 5 AM and the bus driver – the only Finnish bus driver who was not smoking in early 1980s – explained to me in English that some of the tobacconists open their stores at seven, and that would be my chance to buy a new lighter. I had a different idea, though, namely to head towards the campus and ask a local for a light. So I asked the driver to tell me the Finnish words for cigarette lighter and match box. I found his answer both polite in form and essentially callous: "Forget it!". I insisted. He nodded his head disapprovingly. I asked him to write the two words on my bus ticket. He sighed deeply, produced a BIC pen and jotted them down in the following order (I will use capital letters as they must be read with big, really big eyes): SAVUKKEENSYTYTIN (lighter) and TULITIKKULAATIKKO (match). During the next ten minutes, while I was looking for a local smoker who could read my bus ticket, I could have sworn that the driver had actually poked fun of me. After chainsmoking three cigarettes and smothering their strength with the last drops of coffee from my thermos, I picked up my backpack again and started to look for "the many street signs" that were to be found "just everywhere", on which I assumed (after the cigarette lighter & match box experience) I was about to read a word that would look something like "UNIVEERZITTEIKKOINEN". I only saw in that small town lots of blue ONE WAY indicators (many placed in quite bizarre locations), reading the word YLIOPISTO – *"piste unique"*, I imagined an *ad hoc* translation. If you happen to be a polyglot, please think of the word "university" pronounced in all European languages that you speak. Be generous and include here Turkish, Lithuanian and Basque. They won't let you down. Perhaps it is only in the three European Finno-Ugric languages that the bloody word does not start with the U-N-I-V letters. Now, let us see how much these sister-languages resemble each other: university is YLIOPISTO (Finnish), ÜLIKOOL (Estonian) and EGYETEM (Hungarian). Like three quasi-identical dewdrops on a rose petal. My father was right, though: I never saw again the beautiful Hungarian student from the still Yugoslav Croatia. I know from her very lips that in the Croatian language university is called SVEUČILIŠTE – but they also use the word UNIVERZITET. Q. e. d.

Temporalissima was initially sent to our world to learn organ playing. Her melodramatic cover-up was that of a Soviet refugee: a little girl of four or five found near the border and having attached to the interior of her skirt a letter written in a Mordvinian dialect that was related to all these nipple-stiffening languages, known by the name of Erzya (that being the name of the dialect, not of the little girl's). The letter explained that the infant only understands that particular idiom, at a very basic level. It also claimed that her parents lived in the Bashkortostan region before being arrested by the much feared NKVD and sent to an unknown destination (black Volga, prison cell, train, Gulag). Finally, the letter pleaded for the kind of succor that only a kindred nation could provide. It seems that in early 1950s Temporalist exporters suffered from too much imagination.

In her original world, Temporalissima was nineteen years old and the fact that she soon found a Finnish family not reluctant to wipe off her poo represented for the future human calamity the embodiment of the expression "to start off on the right foot" – in a completely new life. She had been previously instructed to pull her adoptive parents' clothes whenever she would pass by a church, to lure them inside with smiles and big-eyed beggings and, if there were organ sounds straining the nave, to produce her first euphoric reaction on Finnish soil. Up to that moment she was supposed to act out the traumatised human pup who wets her underwear whenever knocks on the door are heard after sunset. After a few giggles strategically placed in the insides of a few Lutheran churches, the little girl was bought an upright piano and appointed her first music teacher. Everything was paid for with help from the "Aleksej Vasil'evich Dunyashin" Mordvine Cultural Society from the United States.

When I met her, Temporalissima was, if my deduction is right, around seventy five years old and had the awful habit of speaking her mother tongue with "Europeanized" individuals such as Jean-Philippe or Herr Schaffmann etc. – IF there was nobody around – and in Finnish if a third person would be physically present or at least passing by. If that person did not depart (many actually eavesdropped, as our languages have a very interesting sound for Temporalist ears), our piano player would talk. And talk. And talk. And talk in that language that in its native country is called SUOMALAINEN, hardens the nipples of a certain pharmacy owner and, as far as I understand, is of no use for crossword puzzle amateurs. ("Jet engine specialist", sixty one letters, second down. Hmm... That's a no brainer. It can only be LENTOKONESUIHKUTURBIINIMOOTTORIAPUMEKAANIKK OALIUPSEERIOPPILAS!).

In order to be granted access to her piano and especially (!) to her hand-copied scores, you had to be fluent in one of the European languages, meet her in a public space, and be prepared to listen to her with an approving facial expression, while nodding to this or that unintelligible Scandinavian phrase. That time, the one who sacrificed himself on the Finnish altar was my good friend Jean-Philippe. I was only along the ride in this business. The only word I was able to understand during the forty five minutes of monologue was a "bravo" that Temporalissima once addressed to me for a yet unknown reason.

To make things worse, that day Madame Temporalissima was wearing a meat grinder. My friend addressed her politely in the Temporalist idiom that by that time I was able to represent well enough to spot any kind of irony. There was none. My guide was following her monologue with the utmost attention and only in the rare moments when she stopped to breathe would he discretely and repetitively reformulate our plea to be granted access to "book music instrument welfare harness". That is, roughly, how the concepts would pop up into my consciousness – and mind that it took me no time at all to translate that into "the score of the Well Tempered Clavier".

To those who have read superficially the last paragraph, having actually in mind the image of a meat grinder, I owe an explanation. Madame T. was a beautiful woman, who once had a "generous" body that meanwhile had become slightly "degenerous", if I am allowed the barbarism. In order to compensate that, the pianist used to wear some salopettes made of a fabric that bordered both fishing nets and macramés. The many empty spaces of this knitting allowed not only the skin to breathe, but also the flesh to blossom in thousands of places, like some square fingertips. All this tessellation emanated so much tension that, indeed, the old lady might have been associated with a primaeval explosion of Nature. At a closer examination, though, the tension would lose some of that fleshy prowess and the salopettes indeed looked like the punched metal disks we may observe in meat grinders. One was tempted to position oneself at Madame Temporalissima's back, fit her up with a crank and wind it on until the whole body of the lady would seep through (skin, sinews, flesh, marrow) the eyes of the macramé, eventually becoming a parti-colored mush ready to be introduced into a sheep gut and hanged in a smokehouse.

I am definitely going nuts. It has been three whole days since I started to fill in this notebook, trying to find the right tone for such a difficult subject – and I wasted one precious hour with a rave about stiff nipples, meat grinders and fatcombs. Tomorrow morning, after paying a visit to the pharmacy to announce my employees that they will have to manage things out for a week without their *patron*, I will cross out all these pages and resume the depiction of Temporalist music.

(Summer of 2008)
I should have trashed the last pages. The crossing out was not enough since my wife got literally hysterical: for the past two hours she has laughed continuously and paused only to say that she will divorce me if I dare discard the "Finnish" pages of the last chapter. Any resistance seems futile. Anyway, I put hope in the fact that no editor will ever be so improvident as to publish such a weird book.

(Monday, April the 14th, 2008)
My employees thought I was mad when I told them how happy I was to see them so unchanged after two whole years. The involuntary blunder helped me get an excuse to take the rest of the week off. Wassyla even advised me to stay home "until I feel well again". They were scared probably by the huge dark rings around my eyes. The fourth day at home… It is noon and here I am again, describing my Temporalist journey…

The next day after meeting Madame Temporalissima, Jean-Philippe picked me up from the library and took me for a stroll through the town until we reached the gates of an institution whose social utility remained alien to me. There we were greeted by a tiny Temporalist (the kind of splendid insect, with pearly elytra and beautifully arched feelers who wakes up one morning only to find out that, after an agitated sleep, it has been transformed overnight into a scraggy desk scribbler). The clerk showed us the way to a door and disappeared. In fact, the door was invisible, as it was covered from frame to frame with posters showing our pianist laying down on the piano, resting her left cheek on the keyboard or in "concert position" – with all ten fingers sprawled like the claws of a hawk ready to grasp the white and black sheep spread throughout the eight octaves of the piano.

The "durational music studio" was, thankfully, empty. The focal point was, obviously, the piano itself, along with the many shelves containing hand copied scores painstakingly reproduced from memory, in the last fifty years, by our Finnish speaker. Even the piano bench was covered with a few such manuscripts. Jean-Philippe immediately put them on the stand and started his demonstration:

J.-P.: I asked the lady to pick up for us a set of scores to which the composers did not attach any tempo markings. Here they are. Today we shall make a simple experiment: you will sight-read one work at a time and after a while you will have to decide which is, according to your educated subjectivity, the right tempo. *Tempo giusto*, as it was originally called. Shall we start?

What was initially planned to be a short practical demonstration lingered on for a whole day – and maybe more if the scraggy Temporalist had not rushed in upon the two starving musicians, claiming the room for the right person: Madame Temporalissima was waiting on the hallway, tapping her feet impatiently.

Our game unfolded in the following fashion: I would pick up a composition, read it several times on the keyboard and decide on the right tempo, communicating it to Jean-Philippe who, in his turn, immediately told me which temporal mode the binary or the ternary division of the beat matched – or between which temporal modes it was placed. After this initial stage, my guide helped me find the Temporalist terms to describe why I chose one tempo or another, always taking into consideration the structural components of the respective composition: form, genre, harmonic complexity, intervals, interpretative tradition (or perpetuated bad habits, as they say), polyphonic clarity, temporal harmonization of the different formal sections etc.

For a whole day, therefore (in which we only drank water and shared a thin sandwich) I felt that Temporalist music theory is not only the foundation of an extra-European tradition, but a collection of principles that may very well explain the tempo options for any interpretation of the musical literature that once made me a piano player and transformed Jean-Philippe into a very special cultural hiker.

I could literally fill in dozens of pages with the ideas that popped up around the piano scores hand copied by a human calamity who nevertheless deserved her fair portion of merit. Yet, I would better jot down only those interesting ideas that made me believe for a while that here, in our world, we all are Temporalist musicians who have just not discovered that status as yet.

Madame Temporalissima had the good habit of notating in a separate ledger the tempi chosen by the most appreciated interpreters of a given composer. For instance, all the movements of the 32 Beethoven Sonatas were listed in a table whose header contained names such as Arrau, Fischer, Kempf, Schnabel or Brendel, the columns being carefully filled in with durational values of certain pulsatory layers, minutely scribbled down to milliseconds. This ledger, whose contents only Jean-Philippe was able to decipher, helped us understand why so many times tempo options are not at all "options", but some impositions based on the temporal logic of a given musical composition. The key that unlocked the tempo deduction, my friend convinced me, was not to be found in any book of interpretative theory, and not even in the continuity of the spoken tradition that, for instance, made me a great-grand student of Liszt's and Czerny's. The key, however, was to be found in the basics of Temporalist music theory and, I now dare say, it fit in the sought after keyhole amazingly well.

J.-P.: In order for you to find out the tempo that will eventually self-impose, you must get to "see" the structural temporal elements of any given composition and know the functionality of every conceivable IOI, within and beyond the 50 ms grid, using the perceptual thresholds that were presented to you last year. Here are the defining elements for this particular fugue: the chromatic profile of the eighth notes and the coexistence of both their binary and ternary divisions. Knowing that, please read the fugue until you feel that you have guessed the right tempo.

After a short while, Jean-Philippe announced me that my prolonged contact with Temporalist music did not seem to have passed without consequences, as the tempo I eventually chose was a well defined IOI 150 ms for the ternary sixteenth notes.

J.-P.: Your tempo is both correct and unoriginal. The eighth notes will last for 450 ms each, and that keeps away the risk of being perceived in prosodical groups of two, given the fact that they are placed into an area where the sustainability of attention shift from one pulsation to the next is already well established. It is this very kind of temporal discrimination that was imposed by both the chromatic profile of the eighth notes and their functionality, that is, *basso continuo* without melodic notes. On the other hand, the binary divisions make up a temporal mode that sounds quite strange for a Temporalist ear: IOI 225 ms. These pulsations, considered in groups of two, do not fit in the minimum acton phenomenology, yet they are not sufficiently distanced from it to reach the threshold of the note-by-note processing of isochronous pulsations. The most significant thing in your tempo option is the fact that the binary and the ternary divisions are placed on different sides of the minimum acton threshold, which gives them some very distinctive temporal profiles – and that helps us better distinguish the respective rhythmical layers. If, for instance, you chose IOI 100 ms for the ternary divisions and IOI 150 ms for the binary sixteenth notes, the two modes would have represented instances of the same pulsatory phenomenology whose peak my predecessors initially established at around IOI 120 ms. To say nothing about the fact that, in this tempo, the eighth notes would have occurred every 300 ms, unjustifiably linking the structural chromatic passages of the fugue in groups of two notes each.

No need to say that after that explanation we looked inside Madame Temporalissima's ledger and found for the Well Tempered Clavier a plethora of interpreters, including Feinberg and Hantaï. I remember that my tempo option was identical to that belonging to Davitt Moroney, Glenn Gould and Sviatoslav Richter, and a few milliseconds away from that belonging to Keith Jarrett and Kenneth Gilbert.

Jean-Philippe seemed to be right: there are tempi that somehow self-impose.

(Summer of 2008)

That Monday when I only picked up the pen at around 1:30 PM I was extremely industrious. By the time I fell asleep I managed to fill in no less than 49 pages of such "score analyses". Yet, I do not remember Jean-Philippe ever asking me to transcribe them in this book – not to mention the fact that I do not think I should place such a dissertation under the title I have already chosen for this bizarre book, namely "The Music of the Temporalists". I imagine that those who will read with great attention the chapters of this book that were dictated to me by my two guides will be able to build up themselves the theoretical arsenal necessary to establish the tempo imposed by the texture, genre, interpretative tradition and the rhythmical layers of any given musical composition. None of these can shun the psychoperceptual phenomena that once were presented to me, with so much patience, by a bald musician and an old psychologist. Finally, if by that one chance in a million this book will eventually find a publisher (!) and a large enough public, I could attach in a second edition the score studies that today I decided to eliminate.

(Tuesday, April the 15th, 2008)

It is Tuesday and I am happy that the 13th of this month fell two days ago. The temporal analyses made by Jean-Philippe on Temporalissima's scores represent, therefore, what I could present our musicians with if they were to ask me "what is the use of this theory built up around (or, better said, occasioned by) a musical tradition that is so alien to us?".

J.-P.: It is like that joke (?) about Chinese cuisine: you don't need to speak their language in order to like their food.

I now realize that yesterday I omitted to jot down a few lines about Jean-Philippe's comments on the last five Scriabin piano Sonatas! This Russian musician is considered by the few Temporalists who know of his creation as a composer who was unfortunate enough to be born in the "wrong" musical tradition.

– He should have been one of us, Jean-Philippe whispered to me on one occasion.

134

All notions present in this book and anent to pulsatory grouping theory were introduced to me exclusively by Jean-Philippe during the long period that followed our departure from Herr Professor's house. In order to make things clear from the outset, I must say that no Temporalist musician can claim to master, in its integrality, the art of pulsatory groupings.

When Jean-Philippe taught me how to read Temporalist scores, he also told me that pulsatory groupings initially appeared when composers started to elogize pulsatory structures that they were unable to perform themselves. "To elogize", Herr Schreiber etc. explained to me, means "to imagine" something. The fancy word is necessary because it does not contain the visual connotation of its synonym. People may elogize colors, shapes and smells that they cannot express – or dense orchestral scores written by Richard Strauss, even if they are musically illiterate.

As there are no Temporalist musicians who do not play at least an instrument, the professionalization of these artists is always made hands-on and, after the fourth grade, in a kind of "chamber learning" that I should describe at some point. Here I transcribe a simple example to illustrate what I am about to say:

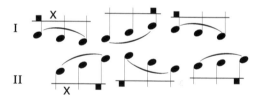

The two students (or more) who are about to perform this pulsatory grouping know that they are not supposed to play two pulsatory voices that incidentally superimpose, but one music that is made of a single temporal mode and whose pulsations no longer comply with the linear TH-AR taxonomy they were used to perform while assimilating the primary modes. In this pulsatory grouping, in which TH and AR values superimpose in multiple contexts, the accent-non-accent dichotomy also has a vertical component. In order to experience it, the two students play alternatively both pulsatory voices. This double "hypostasis", I was told, is essential for the upbringing of young Temporalist interpreters. Without it, musicians would never get to actually elogize the pulsatory groupings.

(Summer of 2008)

After Jean-Philippe presented to me this fifth grade example, I asked him how I could perform, as a simple pianist, such music.

– By automatization and by a kind of intentionality "doppelgänging", was his answer. Listen carefully to Glenn Gould's recordings and you will see that nothing seems impossible.

Interpretative role interchange is a common practice amongst Temporalists precisely because it helps them elogize pulsatory structures in a harmonic manner – that is, vertically. (I can only imagine that our, say, clarinetists find equally useful to know which harmonic progressions their melodic line helps create.)

J.-P.: Imagine that a musical composition is a chess game – that is, already known – played with two or three sets of pieces, white, black and gray, and by as many players. The aim of this game is not winning, but the mental encompassment of all the strategies: the player behind the white pieces should have played before both the black and the gray ones.

Repeated over the years, this practice leads to the creation of a certain type of temporal hearing that is the main "culprit" for the fact that Temporalist musicians possess a quite different brain, trained to elogize their composers' intricate temporal superimpositions that make up the actual pulsatory groupings, whenever the interpreters see them notated in a score – and imagine music graphically upon listening to it.

All these competencies, though, started to be cultivated at a later stage of Temporalist music history. Pulsatory groupings history retained the fact that, in the beginning, composers simply elogized pulsatory structures that they were unable to perform themselves. I will illustrate such a structure with an example taken from the same fifth grade manual that Jean-Philippe provided me with at some point:

As I have mentioned in the chapter dedicated to *acciaccaturas*, the IOI 100 ms temporal mode does not allow for the note-by-note crushing of its pulsations. As a matter of consequence, the above example cannot be performed – yet it may be elogized. Musicians were not content with this paradox and started to de-compose the structures that were inaccessible for one interpreter into several temporal voices that would eventually recompose, for the listeners, the previously elogized music:

136

Students who managed to assimilate accurately the primary temporal modes, in virtually any context and in spite of any disturbances, now have the opportunity to put at work all these abilities. At first, one of the two voices is performed by the Temporal Harmony teacher him- or herself. After a while, the young musicians are encouraged to master this essential task themselves, in small study groups. Pulsatory groupings evolved and complexified constantly. Their performance usually requires the joint contribution of many interpreters: usually three or four – up to seven or even eight. More temporal voices, even if their purpose is to create just one pulsatory grouping, are hard to follow. Whenever I had to listen such temporal "clusters" I recalled some of the stuffy and quasi-ignored Prokofiev Symphonies.

(Summer of 2008)
I remember that upon writing the last paragraph I hesitated whether or not to write about the fact that pulsatory groupings, apart from demonstrating the measure of Temporalist composers' and interpreters' mastership, if written and performed with sufficient talent, sound so bloody well! I will never forget those recordings that I would play over and over again, as if they were pop music hits. I really enjoyed an art that has so little in common with what we call "music".

By the time their composers reached a kind of summit in imagination and sophistication – a period that corresponds roughly to our long and varied Romantic era – compositions were made entirely of pulsatory groupings. Simple, double or triple temporal modes or pulsatory passages written as such for a solo performance became rare and were seen rather like some quotations from the past. While listening to that music, I often thought that I could not have imagined something like it, ever. I therefore asked Jean-Philippe how I was supposed to present the pulsatory groupings given the fact that I was never taught the discipline that tries to organize this art, that is, Temporal Harmony.
– You have no chance to learn this art before forming the necessary neuronal circuits, which can only be achieved by constantly practicing our music, my guide said, cutting short my eagerness.

J.-P.: Our interest is that you present to your people the basics of our musical tradition. We only intend to build a small bridge between two great musical cultures and the best currency for this investment, we think, is the elementary theory of temporal modes. These, like some spermatozoon, contain all the necessary ingredients for a later development if inseminated into the right egg cells, that is, into those minds that are prone to speculative ramifications. We also hope that you graft your amazing talent for pitches onto the ABC of our theory, just as we intend to do the same thing the other way round. I suggested that you get familiar with our musical literature not for a later description of it in your book, but in order to help you explain the theory that made all that music possible from the standpoint of a person who has no doubt that our tradition actually exists. It was for similar reasons that I moved you from one music school to another. Now you know that behind scores and recordings there is a craft that is very hard to achieve, yet it is as real as the fact that you did not sleep at all in the past eighteen months, without feeling drowsy even for a minute.

It was then that I told Jean-Philippe that I wouldn't be able to refrain myself from writing about Temporalist music history and about the way this tradition modified its stylistic profile from one generation to another.

J.-P.: As long as your book will stir the interest of your musicians for a perceptual approach towards musical time, in which durations and pulsatory functions are no longer deduced by augmentations, equivalences and diminutions, but rather by their psychophysical fingerprint – feel free to write about any topic that you think is worth mentioning. For a start, I would be content to see that your musicians start wondering as to what perceptual threshold or thresholds influence one pulsation or another. Later on, some will probably become interested in assimilating the primary modes. That is, to recognize and produce them – and even to learn how to switch from one such mode to another in fewer and fewer steps. Starting from these basics, maybe some musicians will want to improvise some derivative pulsatory structures that won't outline any tempo and won't sound like some *tempi rubati* – but create the first version of our music in your world. There is also the possibility that someone might start juxtaposing different pulsations taken over from the inventory of our temporal modes and produce them at first with help from a computer, at a later stage trying to repeat the resulting structures on a musical instrument. The continuous struggle with the many impossibilities and difficulties posed by pulsatory structuring constituted for us too an inexhaustible source of inspiration and, actually, the basis of our understanding of the ways we are allowed to relate speculatively to discrete time. Perhaps your book will pass unnoticed during your lifetime,

138

but let us hope that in a few generations somebody will pick it up from an old bookshop and use its contents in a way that we cannot even imagine today. Perhaps that musician will be Chinese or Brazilian. Or perhaps he or she won't be a musician at all, but an individual interested, like our philosophers, in the realm of temporal possibility. For all these reasons, I think it will be a futile task trying to explain to your people the way the art of pulsatory groupings have evolved in a distant culture. Let things move at their natural pace and do not try to present some tenth century monodists with the vocal arrangement of a Take Six piece.

I only now realize that from the three examples that I transcribed at the beginning of this chapter someone could imagine that pulsatory groupings are some isochronous structures that cannot be performed by a single instrumentalist. In fact, most pulsatory groupings are not isochronies. Many times pulsatory structures migrate from one temporal voice to another and from one mode to another:

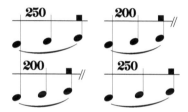

In the "classical" era of Temporalist music, when the art of pulsatory groupings had not yet started to aim specifically at impressing an audience that would come to a concert as if to a continuous magic show, any juxtaposition of two TH values in a time span that was smaller than 400 ms was, most times automatically, distributed to the available temporal voices:

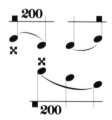

Here are just two of the "good old practices" established during that period which constitute the object of study for Pulsatory Harmony – a discipline that I managed to get familiar with at a very superficial level. Jean-Philippe told me that trying to deepen my understanding would be pointless, as, at its core, it is a combination of both aesthetic and psychoperceptual conditionals.

J.-P.: I am sure you will manage to invent your own canons, if the necessity for that arises. Sooner or later any new art form trains its battalions of scholarly mediocrities who do not have any other purpose but to establish rules and to sanction, *ex cathedra,* those who do not obey them.

The art of pulsatory groupings explains the fact that instrumentalists look at each other so intently during rehearsals and concerts. In the absence of the metrical frame, performers not only prepare their attacks in accordance with the temporal phrases that just unfold, but also permanently elogize their colleagues' parts. Most times, temporal music is a team effort. Authentic pulsatory groupings (if I am allowed to use such a concept) make solitary practice pointless. I suppose that it is for this reason that I have only held in my hands scores containing all the temporal voices involved. Jean-Philippe reminded me of the jugglers who pass clubs and balls, catching and throwing them in the same time.

J.-P.: What kind of "individual study" can that imply?

While I lived amongst Temporalists, it was fashionable to allot pulsatory groupings to the same kind of musical instrument. The timbral non-differentiaton augmented indeed the magic of their music. If you were in a concert hall, you would close your eyes and imagine that only one instrumentalist (not two or three) was able to master all those inimitable pulsatory structures. The great maestros of pulsatory groupings knew how to superimpose such "packages" in a temporal polyphony to which, I am afraid, we won't be granted access any time soon, even if, from my guides' point of view, the fate of this book turns out to be extremely auspicious.

While listening for the umpteenth time to such a composition, I experienced for the first time the horrific feeling that one day I would return to Paris and… I would *never* come across this kind of music again. Well, while writing these very words, I am still capable of elogizing that wonderful piece of music in its entirety.

Before the outbreak of the Brain Revolution, two things marked in a major way the intellectual evolution of Temporalist music: pulsatory groupings and the 50 millisecond grid. Although the former preceded the latter, the idea of speculative development of music only became a common practice the moment the two joined to form a new kind of musical art. That happened less than five centuries ago. Until then, and in the transition century that followed, musicians still used the "natural" temporal modes, more or less rhapsodic forms, and a subtle art of allusions that united musical pulsations with speech. The latter, even if it did not bore me to death, was too fuzzy for my ears (the same ears that never helped me utter a single intelligible Temporalist word). But maybe I was unable to develop the type of sensibility necessary to enjoy Temporalist music written before the implementation of the 50 ms grid. The fact that restitutive consorts like that of Jean-Philippe's son are so successful should have made me reconsider the sheer subjectivity by which I now dismiss the music of a few important musical generations. Anyway, if I were to chose between our Gregorian monodies and the old Temporalist music, I would undoubtedly be inclined to prefer the latter.

Some six hundred years before my temporary journey on Temporalist soil, the musicians from a certain town that we briefly visited began to quarrel. Some wanted to perform the old "My lass is soft like a sweetbread", whereas others wanted to perform for the eighth time "The naughty carpenter", a new hit. Jean-Philippe assured me that, if the symbology anent to the two compositions ever circulated in Europe during the 15th century, those musicians would have ended up burnt at the stake.

While still heckling and disputing, one of them pounded the table with a stony fist and thunderously shouted a title that dropped onto the head of Temporalist music history like that apple that met Sir Isaac Newton: "The naughty carpenter wants to taste the sweetbread of my lass".

– What is that? the other musicians asked, seconds before starting to go together by the ears.

– That means… we can perform both pieces at the same time, said the man who had just launched the strange title. Let the noisiest team win!

History did not record how much alcohol was involved in that contest – only the fact that, while our carpenter enjoyed his lasses' raisins, something went terribly right. Everybody felt the magical flash of the first pulsatory grouping – as the anecdote goes. More than that, someone had the talent or the divine inspiration to remember precisely the moment of that uncanny temporal incidence brought about by the flutter of an angel's wings.

(Summer of 2008)
My wife just asked me what I had to drink before writing the last sentences. I think it was some cheap Italian table wine that failed to tenderize some veal shins.

It took just one more generation for Temporalist musicians to make the complete transition from superimposing some already known musical pieces to the creation of those verticalized temporal structures that later will bear the name of "pulsatory groupings". The moment coincided with the first claims for a temporal grid able to clarify the way those verticalizations were supposed to sound, without the need for the small instrumental ensembles to meet and make repertorial exchanges. The solution – that is, the 50 ms grid – would have to wait another hundred years before becoming the standard.

During all of this period, a lot of music was performed – but, unlike in the European tradition, no composer's name was ever mentioned. There were indeed myriad ensembles that, instead of rehearsing and offering public concerts, just kept alive the temporal verticalization hobby. Back then, effectology was priced better than formal coherence. The most impressive pulsatory groupings created by means of this joint effort were consequently placed in some expository frames and or within small, repetitive loops that were rhetorically interchanged.

I now realize that Jean-Philippe was actually right when he advised me to let my fellow musicians discover for themselves, in time, the art of pulsatory verticalizations. As long as musical pulsations do not bear in my world the same significances that Temporalists know so well, my attempt indeed may seem pointless. Yet, after reading the previous paragraph again and again for some fifteen minutes, – and after absentmindedly doodling half of this page – I decided to continue, assuming the risk of a failed attempt.

During that period, their musical world was circulated by various musical formulae that – had they been melodic and not pulsatory in nature – would have had the formal functionality of our musical motifs. Their "meaning" was based on the gestural rhetorics of a just constituted tradition that managed to become, in just a short time, the *lingua franca* of a quite large musical community. Just as, while listening to an Alberti bass or an organ point, we will never assume we are dealing with the first theme of a Viennese Sonata, those many pulsatory formulae that circulated in those years in the Temporalist world had precise formal functions, confirmed by repetition and recognizable as such. This rhetorical arsenal is no different, at its core, from the poïetical tricks of the European musical tradition. This is why it was not so hard for me to adapt my listening strategies: after just a few weeks of continuous contact with Temporalist music, I knew what was important to follow and how to discern hierarchically the structures of a given composition.

What remains highly original in Temporalist music is the moment of "formal jubilation", which is neither a well-knit stretto, nor a speculative clash of some thematic materials previously exposed. Their tradition came up with these verticalizations, in which already exposed pulsatory structures do not melt together in a kind of creative compromise and do not interchange motivically. They remain roughly unchanged, but disappear in a kind of background the moment they are combined in pulsatory groupings, as the latter suddenly seize the relevant foreground of educated listeners' perception.

(Summer of 2008)
I have just read the last pages – and I am not at all content with my attempt to describe Temporalist music, yet I have no idea how I should accomplish this task in a better way. I feel like a Japanese explaining to some Mormon missionaries why he and his fellow citizens cry while reading a text about the way moonlight reflects off the shiny skin of a tsuchi-gaeru frog.

At some point, the Temporalist musical community started to get bored with the "pulsatory structures first exposed and then verticalized, at once or in several stages" formula. More and more members of the old instrumental ensembles discovered that their elogization capabilities had sharpened to such a degree that they were able to dream of "compositional cathedrals" (Jean-Philippe's term) in which they superimposed not just some simple temporal voices, but whole packages of already verticalized pulsatory groupings: a combination of big-band and fast-food that introduced the names and surnames of composers in the history of Temporalist music. At the same time, excessive verticalizations turned the 50 ms grid into today's standard.

The decisive step towards the new style was made when an ambitious organologist reminded musicians that they were endowed with two hands and, as a matter of consequence, they could produce some fine verticalizations in the solitude of their own homes, provided they had the necessary resources to purchase a copy of the instrument the organologist just brought to perfection: the whakerbaleen. (The name of the instrument is my invention and represents the syllabic acronym of "whale keratin baleen".) The 180-200 keys of the instrument are about three millimeters thick, each corresponding to a certain pitch. Obviously, every finger stroke pushes down more than one key, yet an ingenious mechanism only lets one sound be produced and consequently heard.

Jean-Philippe pointed out to me that a whakerbaleenist can verticalize only some of the pulsatory structures that two interpreters usually are able to perform. At the same time, some of the solo verticalizations invented by the most talented whakerbaleenists cannot be performed by other instrumentalists, not even by a joint effort. This instrument modified to such an extent the social profile of those who dedicated their lives to it that even I can distinguish, in a room crammed with Temporalist musicians, the ethereal countenance of the whakerbaleenists.

Initially there was a period defined by the sentence "dear composer, we cannot perform something like that with our instruments". You might have already guessed that whakerbaleenists were artists prone to creative ambitions – while the old composers also adopted, with gusto, the new instrument. The former, not having sufficiently experienced orchestral practice, started to elogize verticalizations that tended to have little in common either with the old tradition or the very temporal competence that an instrumentalist was supposed to have achieved. Things happened for a while in the following way: the composer, who had just dismantled a whakerbaleen while composing a "cathedral", would commission an orchestra to perform it. Instrumentalists would look over the score and start to backpedal, saying that such intricacies were way above their humble skills. Two more stages would follow: bringing the whakerbaleen to the orchestra, and the magic trick by which an octopus demonstrates to a congregation of earthworms that eight arms may be coordinated quite well.

All these skirmishes ebbed away by the time it was determined that, no matter how complicated the pulsatory cathedrals may look, they ought to obey the 50 ms grid that just found the perfect time for a definitive implementation. The moment coincided with the creation of the first music academies on Temporalist soil, founded by a small number of whakerbaleen virtuosi, who managed to convince some wealthy ladies to use their fortunes for a noble purpose. The ladies, who appreciated these Lisztian maestros for more than their artistic qualities, were eager to put their resources into these historical endowments and contribute to the implementation of the whakerbaleen as the standard instrument in Temporalist musical education. I have seen king-size versions of this instrument in virtually every living room, even if most of the amateur performers were actually psychologists. All instrumentalists know how to play it to a certain degree, as it is used for the teaching of Temporal Harmony in all superior stages of musical education.

The 50 ms grid, in combination with the first musical instrument that allowed composers to perform some pulsatory verticalizations themselves, have defined the beginning of the "classical" period in Temporalist music. Paradoxically, it was then that composers obsessed with temporal cathedrals started to vanish, along with the vanity of showing how many pulsatory voices one may meaningfully superimpose. Instead, simple works for solo instruments accompanied by the whakerbaleen became very popular. If it were not from such a different culture, I would be tempted to say that Temporalists had just invented the Sonata. As many of the generous ladies played one of the old instruments themselves, whakerbaleen composers hurried to dedicate to them elaborate works that were extremely difficult technically, so that a great number of rehearsals were required before the first public performance. To this day the music of that period is mainly cultivated by couples: a female soloist and a male whakerbaleenist.

Most times, at the beginning of such a "Sonata", the solo instrument outlines a sinuous temporal track in which IOIs change a lot and where larger, compound modes abound. In a deliberate way, "the audience is invited to understand little or nothing" (Jean-Philippe's words) from the respective pulsatory structures, except for the fact that at some point it gets repeated, this time joined by a contrapuntal accompaniment from the whakerbaleenist that clarifies some of the thesis-arsis dichotomies of the apparently formless initial exposition. By this first verticalization, the "theme" is considered exposed and starts to sound meaningful to the audience. Yet it will not be repeated until the end of the composition, before that being redrawn in smaller segments that are verticalized either directly, or progressively. This middle section roughly corresponds to the idea of thematic development from our musical tradition. Step by step, listeners will start to associate certain pulsatory structures (performed either by the soloist or by the whakerbaleenist) with certain verticalizations, so that by the end of the performance, when the "theme" is finally repeated, it looks somehow confirmed, justified and fully meaningful. As a kind of coda, the instrumentalists abandon the pulsatory superimpositions and re-expose the series of pulsations that the composition started with – which will remain as formless for the perception of a music lover who has just entered the concert hall, and will be fully clarified for those who have followed the whole musical plot.

I have no idea what I could compare these Temporalist "Sonatas" to. An utmost ambiguity that has to be justified progressively and placed in a clarifying context. It is like a strange melody that doesn't let us easily guess its possible harmonizations, discern its tonality, differentiate its diatonics from its chromatics – and which, with help from a harmonic

145

instrument such as the piano, is step by step bound by the stylistic harnesses of tonal harmony (as the latter was structured at a given historical period).

I have just tossed the die (in fact, a die-shaped candle, a benign kitsch brought by my wife from Mexico). I had just wasted an hour trying to exemplify the way such a pulsatory "enigma" gains in consistency by those progressive verticalizations. On the one hand, I am simply unable to bring zeuxilogic notation to this level of intricacy. On the other, I wonder what I should do with these large examples if a publishing house will ever want to print the book. So – I took the die and said: if I throw a six, I will include such examples in this book. It was a three. Hallelujah!

The Temporalist "Sonata" was readily embraced by the public, while the formal avatars of this new musical genre soon mushroomed in the most unexpected ways. Much in vogue was a composition whose initial solo exposition was not only formally clear and unambiguous, but sounded very much like the old pulsatory structurings that were all the rage during the chamber consorts period. The middle, developmental section revealed the fact that those apparently clear pulsatory structures may be verticalized in spite of the initial perception. One was made to wonder what the significance of the initial structure was. A caterpillar who dies a butterfly or a butterfly who was once born a caterpillar? Since in Temporalist music history no simple and beautiful thing is meant to last forever, pulsatory structures were invented allowing for two or even three distinct verticalizations. The lady soloists had to find other pretexts to meet their whakerbaleenist lovers once the orchestral ensembles again became fashionable, while taking over the new verticalization techniques.

Once again, to my humble knowledge, this strange way to envisage musical composition – the transformation of a unshapely, "ugly", aberrant musical material into something limpid – finds no equivalent in the history of European music, which witnessed both lyrical embodiments and epic constructions but was never assimilated extensively to riddles (although Bach, with his *Kleines Harmonisches Labyrinth,* might have been of a different opinion). On the other hand, leaving aside the idea of clarification, often times Baroque fugue subjects were thought of along with a matching countersubject and with the possible architecture of a consequent *stretto.* Our composers' ability to see the countersubject of a fugue in its subject and vice versa reminds me of the old Temporalist art of extracting "deformities" from well structured pulsatory verticalizations

146

and placing the former at the beginning of the composition, for a later "repair".

After a few decades, representatives of the new generations got sick of all these riddles, perhaps the same way that, in the late 1700s, the Mannheim symphonists discarded for good polyphonists' *basso continuo*. Many verticalizations from the middle sections of Temporalist "Sonatas" sounded amazingly well. Composers reached such a degree of professionalism that they were able to elogize and put on paper some really magical temporal formulae while the public, utterly enchanted by these, started to ignore the formal solidity of this new music, waiting for the pulsatory fireworks that had just became the equivalent of Farinelli's roulades. More and more music lovers filled the concert halls, while the music itself, obeying the popular taste, started to tolerate mediocrity to an extent hitherto unheard of. The old introductions lost their initial expository role and became a mere term of comparison for the virtuoso passages that were supposed to "murder" them afterwards. I use this harsh term just because the old composers, who had partially given up their integrity in order to keep their audience, were unable to cope anymore with the speed at which good taste was becoming more and more obsolete. This was the context that allowed for the emergence of the first musical "killers" – a bunch of well-versed improvisers who exposed pulsatory structures with the only purpose of verticalizing them with virtuosity, the same way one is "verticalized" by a bomb that has just blown up under one's arse.

If the superficies of musical life was confiscated by these talented mountebanks, somewhere in the middleground, the world of the orchestras adopted the Temporalist "Sonata" genre and continued to support a handful of composers who considered the whakerbaleen "a disgrace and the main culprit for the fact that musicians' relation with discrete time has reached such levels of vulgarity".

Jean-Philippe explained to me that, in reality, the "orchestra composers" copied or simply stole lots of compositional techniques from those "bad taste mongers". They too gave up the old musical riddles and replaced them with the old dilemma: does my music sound well or does it sound bad? For this reason, orchestral compositions from that era started to resemble, at least apparently, the European musical rhetorics of the Romantic period. Temporalists had just discovered the idea of "thematic material," and even the concept of "thematic development". Whereas pulsatory groupings had hiterto helped the clarification of the apparently shapeless expository section, as the latter disappeared, composers chose to keep a good grip on their audiences by playing with expectations and listening strategies that were sometimes confirmed and other times shunned or even wrapped up as unexpected confirmations. While listening to this music, my ears always felt "at home", as I recognized the old tricks used by our own composers. Jean-Philippe confirmed my intuition and told me that at some point he even dedicated a seminar to these intercultural (or even inter-paradigmatic – sound versus pulsation) resemblances, the pretext being the theoretical work of a German musicologist whose name was totally unknown to me – Heinrich Schenker.

If I am not wrong, it was during that period too that verticalizations started to "horizontalize". That is not an oxymoron, but a reality imposed by the instrumentalists' high degree of professionalization, as by that time they were the second or third generation of music academy graduates. Music teaching became a discipline itself and the advanced students were extremely skillful with temporal modes, passages and the art of pulsatory groupings. The latter's old definition was "a pulsatory structure that can be obtained only by the *superimposition* of two or more intentionalities" (i.e. temporal voices). Most times, the pulsatory structure outlined by each voice posed no technical difficulty to the professional interpreters. Problems started to emerge with the placement of these structures into the verticalized universe of pulsatory groupings, where all the perturbing elements appeared: inertiae and jammings that had to be surpassed in order to achieve the feeling that, by verticalization, voices become a new instrument, producing a new music. For better coordination, often times voices evolved into short synchronous passages. Thus interpreters assured themselves that the temporal modes just being played were kept on the right track. Well, the first university graduates started to feel somehow offended by the fact that scores were in no shortage of such helpful coincidences, which in their view were just scholastic tricks dating back from the years when whakerbaleenists composed Sonatas having in mind the temporal abilities of their wealthy mistresses.

So, the validity of the old definition was still in place, yet it was amended with a new technique that was formulated as "a linear pulsatory structure that can be obtained only be *alternating* two or more intentionalities". The role-interchange practice appeared just because of this technique. Most times two musicians playing the same instrument would perform a score that neither one could play alone. If you are in a concert hall or if you listen to a recording, you will perceive only one instrument that gives life to a series of "impossible" linear pulsatory structures. The effect is often times magical and the trick behind the smoke curtain, although most times the same, was reinvented compositionally in more and more elaborate forms.

148

As our brain cannot produce or anticipate but a single main accent per acton or a single accent per minimum acton, this perceptual configuration was thwarted speculatively by alternating two or more interpretative intentionalities. I transcribe below a simple yet highly illustrative example:

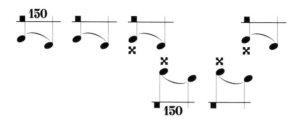

Over only 600 ms, listeners' brains are made to perceive four TH values, instead of three hierachized accents, two unsustainable accents or one sustainable accent. Add to that the effort of quite a few generations to sublimate the magic of this trick to a higher level of sophistication, the contribution of two or three geniuses and listeners' appetite for pulsatory structures that may be elogized, but cannot be performed as such. (In the same way we may elogize orchestral music without having any means to produce it by ourselves.)

As whakerbaleenists were unable to improvise anything similar to the most elaborate horizontalized pulsatory groupings, their glory days ebbed away and musical good taste started to matter again in the world of those preoccupied with the evolution of their own musical culture.

Moreover, as the new style produced scores for whose interpretation individual study was most times pointless, musical ensembles became either some sort of family business or some bizarre communities (at least in my view) – a kind of quasi-tribal guild in which free sex brought about social cohesion and diffuse parental responsibilities. Those people, I was told, would stop from their musical activities only if they were hungry or if their children would get mortally sick. If the children survived infancy, there was always a generous sponsor to adopt the most talented ones and send them to one of the boarding schools for young performers. After that, the musicians would either marry or join another musical "tribe", as instrumentalists or composers.

J.-P.: Not in a thousand years will European civilization be able to produce something similar, if you adopt our musical theory. All our musicians possess a temporal perception that is modified by the continuous contact with the specificities of our musical tradition. Those people, though, almost became a different species. If it were not for discrete time perception, but for smell, I could have compared them with your sniffer dogs. Who knows? Maybe one day we shall discover that a kind of genetical mutation took place in the bosom of these communities, because I find it hard to imagine another explanation for the fact that, even after this kind of social structure disappeared, their descendants still possess a native predisposition for music. Whereas in your world you cannot muster one hundred top violin players without noticing that perhaps three quarters of them are or were of Jewish origins, something similar happens here with the descendants of those musical "tribes".

(Summer of 2008)
Come to think of it, many of the artists that I came across in concert halls and universities had those typical "Temporalist musician faces" – a prejudice that was not inculcated into my relational perception by anybody, but was created by sheer evidence. I still wonder if they were the descendants of those strange guilds about whose former existence Jean-Philippe had told me.

For a lengthy period, Temporalist music became stabilized – meaning that scores generally looked the following way: each sound register was covered by a group of two or three interpreters playing the same kind of instrument. Within these compartments, (superimposed) verticalizations were not allowed. Only horizontal pulsatory groupings were written, while it became an accepted practice to continue (as a prolonged sound) the last pulsation attacked by the instrumentalist who just "relayed" to his or her colleague. Nobody viewed that as a type of verticalization, but as a mere stylistic license that, to this day, is regarded as secreting the scent of a certain historical period. Verticalizations only took place at an inter-compartmental level. Thus, all pulsatory structures by which composers tried to display their craftsmanship became something that a single interpreter, such as a whakerbaleenist, could not perform at all.

Simple pulsatory structures, though not necessarily lacking a degree of technical difficulty, never disappeared from Temporalist music. I refer to those instrumental parts for the interpretation of which the individual study was not at all pointless. Many works commenced with such *captatio benevolentiae* introductions, while the more elaborated sections of some compositions were many times followed by formal resolutions built up by means of some pulsatory structures that created no pulsatory groupings, either horizontally, or vertically.

In comparison to our music history, the concerto genre appeared much later. The idea of "soloist" was nefariously associated to the infatuated whakerbaleenists and the mistresses of their predecessors. All instrumentalists were used to studying along with their compartment colleague or colleagues and consequently to participating in the final orchestral rehearsals. The very thought that such a performer could play a leading role looked for many decades as something alien to a musical tradition that had just started to get old. On the other hand, the habit of sending the most talented children of the indifferent mothers and uncertain fathers to study in the best Temporalist musical establishments looked very much like the French colonialist custom of kidnapping children from the African tribes, educating them in missionary environments and sending them back after a decade as vectors of civilizing influence. These educated musicians no longer believed that excellence was achieved by simply playing the instrument for ten to twelve hours daily. During summer holidays, they would return to their original "tribes" only to notice that they were regarded as some celebrities just because they always brought with them novelties, knew many unheard of fiddly tricks and carried along with them some state-of-the-art or newly invented instruments.

This particular detail would soon give birth to a wholly new musical genre, invented by these educated artists themselves. Their instruments covered four-five octaves, every register being tuned like certain traditional instruments, so that the upper notes would nicely fit with the sopranino trombflute, the middle register with the violoboe, while the lower pitches were a perfect match for the counterpiccolo (or whatever names Temporalist instruments actually have). During the long summer days, such an instrumentalist would hardly find a place for him- or herself in the "tribal" orchestras that ceaselessly rehearsed or performed – and that is why the first compositions to make the most of their special skills were soon introduced into the Temporalist repertory.

By the time the Temporalist concerto became as popular as any other musical genre, the soloist part looked like a kind of "glue". The general rule was that the different instrumental compartments do not produce structurally important verticalizations without the participation of the *obbligato* instrument that would either soar to the treble to contribute to the exposition of a linear pulsatory grouping, help build some verticalizations in the middle register or introduce some new thematic material in the baritonal range. If all this working bee effort did not take place at a pulsatory level but within our classical tradition, the soloist would have been a kind of handyman who here clarifies an ambiguous harmonic function and there finishes off a pulsatory structure, while in between he continues to expose the new pulsatory motives that the orchestra would take over and dismantle with a kind of awkwardness that was attentively planned ahead by the composer.

151

And then... less than 150 years ago, the civilization that invented a musical system hitherto never related to psychology or the brain sciences – suddenly discovered the New World. Not at the other end of a vast ocean, but inside the skulls of these gray skinned humans. From that point and until the day I returned to Paris to write this book, the Brain Revolution represented the only major concern of Temporalist society. Inevitably, the classical period of Temporalist music came to a halt. In the following century, temporal modes were discovered within their psychophysical framework, which was attached to them quite forcibly, although, evidently, musicians could have perpetuated their tradition without this scholarly sophistication. Yet, to be honest about Temporalist history, nothing escaped the revolutionary spree.

The chronology of the impact inflicted upon the old musical tradition is much too eventful. During the four or five succeeding generations, music lovers' profiles changed radically. Whereas before the turning point orchestras lured in the concert halls a macédoine of craftsmen, clerks, musicians and teenagers – after the Revolution, half of the concertgoers were somehow related to the new disciplines. The tota tea, soup or pill was now being given to three-year-old children (or even younger toddlers) and thus their life expectancy, although more or less the same, was enriched with a much longer active (and not slept) life. Children's extra time was unexpectedly dedicated to the arts – especially to music, an art that was considered a living proof of the ways the human brain can be optimized.

From the very dawn of the Brain Revolution, psychologists started to desire to be musicians, and musician – psychologists. This indecisive marriage was in fact the incubator that hatched all those poets and philosophers, plus other species of academic animals, each one murkier than the next. Jean-Philippe himself has a kind of MD in brain sciences, while the young Herr Schlang etc. studied the whakerbaleen for many years before discovering that a Bavarian chalet cannot be achieved by performing pulsations in front of an audience composed of parents, relatives and other amiable guests. Jean-Philippe confessed that he sometimes loathes the world that he was destined to live in. He was lucky, though, to have met an admirable woman who gave birth to two nice and loving children. Then, his life changed dramatically when he contacted the music of a parallel world, first discovered in the memories of some Temporalists whose consciousnesses had been exported to several of our big cities, only to return fraught with such collateral surprises.

As in our own world, music academies became more and more open to logical positivism or analytical intellectualism and quite intolerant with divergent thought and unsophisticated talent. The career of a musician affiliated to a Temporalist university is more likely assessed in written dissertations than in public performances. In the brunt of all these transformations, music became a thousand new things that were equally interesting and unappealing. In order to describe them, I should have to know their chronology and be able to write down the names of the composers who transformed an old musical tradition into a lofty dialogue with their own psychotemporal competencies.

Whereas one hundred years after the outbreak of the Brain Revolution Temporalist music was still defined by schools and trends, from that moment on aesthetically unaffiliated composers became the norm. As challenging the limits of the discrete-temporal perception did not require the expressive vector of pitches, many psychomusicians started to tap their ideas on the table. One of these erudites even claimed that sound is a mere ornament that, indeed, bestows a certain meaning upon the pulsatory structures but, at another level, creates as much confusion. This is how the first percussion instruments penetrated Temporalist music.

Another musician, who had the bad habit of attaching an explanatory book to every composition he wrote, decided that the idea of a public concert is an act of vanity in itself and that music should only get to our brains visually, as a printed score, only consequently being elogized by musicians' educated perception. "After all, storytellers do not need their works to be recited on stage – why should composers remain the beneficiaries of this never amended special treatment?" This manifesto was completely ignored by actual musicians, yet embraced by those scholars who were mostly preoccupied with the universe of temporal possibility.

Jean-Philippe told me that in the past seventy or so years Temporalist music evolved on a path that was strangely similar to the history of our contemporary music. The old tradition was "vandalized" the same way a furious mob may vandalize a trolley bus trying to cross a riotous square. One revolutionary composer removed its headlights, another one the seats, while the third took the ticket punchers… and so on. Upon bringing home all these trophies, each one continued his or her own revolution starting from the respective object. In our world, Jean-Philippe claims, there are countless such composers "who dismantled the trolley bus". He enumerated for me perhaps a dozen categories – I had heard about minimalists but nothing about "spectralists" (?).

In their world, Temporalist composers followed the common places of a similar revolutionary project. One such "path opener" wanted to show how ambiguous the thesis-arsis dichotomy may get at the level of a single moment of incidence. His music displays many such time points, where four or five TH and AR pulsations coincide, none of which having the same prosodical configuration.

Despite the fact that the idea of "trendiness" was permanently discredited by psychomusicians, for a while it was extremely trendy to use those bus parts defined by long durations, taken from the IOI 800-2000 ms range. In the Temporalist world, a new trend is established the following way: several composers steal at the same time the repetitive inventory of the trolley bus – seats, tires or windows. A period of tension follows, when everyone claims that they were imitated or plagiarized by some unimaginative pasticheurs. The first ones who plant the flag on the new trend jubilate. The others get frustrated and claim to have actually kept deep in a drawer the scores proving that the great music of the bus rims was actually their invention. Thus, the scandal establishes the new trend.

Such an invention, simultaneously invented by dozens of composers who still dispute its paternity, was "the present time music". By that time, psychologists had just succeeded in eluding perceptual present in their laboratories. The "now" moment could mean several time-spans. Their relationship with actons and short time memory could incorporate a whole new range of connotations. Thus, a new music emerged, in which the public, in order to understand what was going on, had to refresh from time to time its own "present moment". I had the opportunity to attend a few concerts of such presentualist (?) music. Every 400-3000 ms, a percussion instrument marks for the audience the mandatory refreshment of temporal windows. I was informed that the listener will not understand a jot from the musical discourse if he or she doesn't flinch inside with each drumstick hit while imagining that each such signal represents a new, "absolute" start of the music. Theoretically, the compositions were supposed to be reconstructed mentally in the hours following the concert. To be frank, I was never able to perform this listening strategy – yet, no matter my incompetence, "presentualists" were represented by a few undeniable talents whose works I actually enjoyed.

Even if the European musical tradition was first encountered by Temporalist travellers during Leon Blum's first term in office, these mental "excursions" remained top secret until our mid-fifties. After that, Temporalists like Jean-Philippe would return from Europe or America telling everybody that they listened there to a strangely beautiful music that they could not reproduce, performed on some instruments that

154

they were unable to replicate. Until the day Temporalissima built the cloned Olof Granfeldt piano, our music represented to Temporalists a series of brays, impressions and clumsy theoretical descriptions. It was always rumored, though, that "there is something about these sounds". Instrumentalists started to improvise sounds more attentively and discuss terms such as "consonance" and "dissonance". Our musical universe stirred constant interest and inadvertent understanding – but was not able to budge music from its pulsatory-temporal pedestal. Jean-Philippe was still hoping that this event would take place during his lifetime. Numerous macabre innuendos regarding Temporalissima (age, obesity) that my friend would blurt out after a few glasses of "Korean" plum wine made me guess his future plans: the irreparable loss of the great lady would be assuaged by bringing on Temporalist soil a real pianist from our world, one possessing a quasi-exhaustive repertoire and the memory of an Indian elephant.

J.-P.: What a pity Richter is gone. A German with a Slavic soul may squeeze the best from a piano – provided that he lets Johann Sebastian rest in peace…

(Wednesday, April the 16th)

I planned to put an end to this account today. Yesterday I wrote about things that, in my guides' view, should have remained untold. It was only during the night that I realized what an injustice I made to Temporalist music history, how many important events I omitted to mention and how useless are, in the absence of a direct contact with Temporalist music, the descriptions I managed to put on paper.

I was enjoying the hospitality of a small pedagogical centre when Jean-Philippe approached the library desk where I was picking up new recordings – and whispered into my left ear:

– It's over. In a few hours we return home.

I had one more week to spend on Temporalist soil, time that I was invited to waste in the company of Jean-Philippe and his family. It was the "farewell week" that mirrored the "accommodation week" from the beginning of my journey.

The forest in which my friend's home is located was eight or nine walking hours away. We planned to cover half the distance at night, under the stars, and the other half in the morning. It was spring again and the old gig that had carried my things during all my academic roamings was parked on the front lawn of the pedagogical centre. Whenever my guide was unable to join me from one music school to another, the gig was attached to some caravans, while a student would help me pull the chaise that in the end was crammed with souvenirs that I was unable to give away, knowing that they would all remain in Jean-Philippe's home and in my nostalgic thoughts.

On our way back, our discussion jumped quickly from one subject to another. He was once again under the euphoric influence of the "plum wine" that he would drink at every halt. As far as I was concerned, I had discovered a new (and in fact very old) vice that eventually would spread like bush fire throughout the Temporalist academic world…

One night, Jean-Philippe started to count the months remaining up until our parting and, at the end of that, the only thing that he found suitable to tell me was that he envies me for the fact that in less than a year I would again enjoy the scent of a filterless Gauloises inhaled "to the soles". This subject used to scare me because every time I remember the day I quit smoking I feel like recollecting a crime for which I was never punished, but instead praised and encouraged to recount as if it were some sort of meaningful parable. That is like saying that confined soldiers should not be ashamed for being wankers, as long as they do that nasty thing *manu militari*.

As the boxes containing dried out and finely ground tota leaves were always handy, I asked Jean-Philippe whether the smoke resulted from the combustion of the weed was by any chance not stuffy, peppery or smothery. He replied that he had no idea, as he supposed that I did not know what the smell of burnt black tea leaves was. In less than a minute, a small pile of tota leaves was fumigating on a minuscule plate placed between us. To Jean-Philippe, the smell seemed "dubious", while I found it a little bit punchy, yet bearable. That is precisely the way, a long time ago, I perceived the scent of the American cigarettes that my parents had just voluptuously discovered. Risking a severe coughing bout, I decided to take my chance and bent over the smoke with the mouth wide open, inhaling the whitish fluid slowly and equally, until I felt that my lungs were prepared to play the role of a steam engine. While keeping the smoke inside my lungs, I returned to the chair and counted out, like I did when I was a student, up to seven – C-A-N-A-B-I-S –, after which I puffed out the smoke, and for a very short while I clearly saw my Parisian room, where I now write about this uncanny experience.

– Jeannot, I murmured, I think we stand a real chance of winning the next year Nobel Prize for Peace! This weedy weed of yours is simply amazing!

With so many potter shops around, it was not hard for us to describe and order a pair of clay pipes, but the leaves were burning too fast, leaving behind a fine soot that clogged the mortise and the draft hole after the first two minutes of smoking. I asked Jean-Philippe to find the thinnest paper available, and he returned after a couple of hours carrying along with him three pieces of tracing paper. I instantly rolled up three cigarettes and tested each one with great care. One of the papers was clearly imbued with some flammable substance, as it instantly produced a flame that scorched my nostril hairs. The second burned quite well, yet, although transparent, was too thick and smoky. Finally, the third sample burned unevenly, but it was virtually smokeless, so I had to decide in favor of the last brand whose name I consequently carried along with me, written on my "tota purse".

As from outside I looked like any other Temporalist male of my age, up to then I had never been annoyed by too many gawkish looks or gossipy whispers. The day I started to smoke one tota cigarette after every lunch... well, that day completely changed that state of facts. Imagine that you are enjoying your snack and next to you there is this character who pulls out from his lunch pail a huge mechanical alarm clock which he starts to eat while glancing with broody eyes somewhere in the distance. Clock face, cogwheels, complications. That is how I looked in the eyes of the students who stopped to stare at me swallowing tota smoke.

After a few such days, Jean-Philippe told me that students kept asking him what his mute friend was doing. After a week, I ceased to be the only smoker. Two batty girls would wait for me during the lunch break and offer me slim rolled cigarettes filled with a divine blend of tota leaves. By the end of the summer, someone managed to invent the ashtray, while in the air of the university hallways there permanently lingered a fine scent of burnt tota.

The day we started our final trip to Jean-Philippe's home I was able to go to the pedagogical centre "totateteria" and ask for a pack of twenty (!) cigarettes produced by the first specialized factory. The Temporalist fellow whose body I used to wear for two years was probably extremely baffled to see that his mug was printed on some boxes containing some strangely packed tota leaves and that many people who blew smoke out of their mouths were saluting him cordially.

Although an inveterate smoker whenever he returned to Paris, Jean-Philippe considered that my small discovery was no match for the relishes provided by the dark tobacco leaf well blended and packed under the Gauloises Caporal or Obrero labels. The fact is, that day, drinking the "Korean wine" or smoking the tota leaves, we were feeling wonderful while strolling along the dirt roads surrounding the rolling strips of cultivated land. In the hours that followed we discussed many things but, although no more than two weeks have passed since that day, I only remember that, at some point, I asked my friend what I could do if, once returned to Paris and after having written the book for whose completion I had been imported there for two years, I would miss that music to which I was already mentally and spiritually addicted to.

J.-P.: Unfortunately, your visit was not planned to include a practical dimension, as we never intended to transform you into a musician. Let alone that it would have been impossible over only two years. On the other hand, you have assimilated well the basics of our music theory and the thousands of hours you have spent in concert halls, listening to our recordings and following scores – all these made you familiar with the ways our theory may be transposed into actual music. For all these reasons, I believe that the keywords in your case are "improvisation" and "speculation". Starting from the theoretical framework, you could build up various pulsatory juxtapositions, while trying to imagine them mentally or play them on the piano. Conversely, you may try improvising in any of our musical styles and, if your fingers will be able to produce some interesting pulsatory combinations, try putting them on paper, using Herr Professor's zeuxilogic notation. The fact that you have listened to so much music in which the idea of beat is absent may liberate you from this repetitive tic that is so specific to your world.

The important thing is that your extemporizations make some sense at a rhetorical level. Not to mention that in the past twenty years your homes were conquered by the informational revolution and, I can only guess, a computer may be easily made to render the specific durations taken over from our temporal modes. Use that technology, as at first it will be inevitable for you to perform our modes falsely.

Jean-Philippe continued his advice by saying that the great difficulties would only start the moment I would try to perform passages from one temporal mode to another. My brain must get accustomed with short temporal windows, as its natural predisposition is to seek for a kind of "perceptual rest" after each elogized or produced acton. In order to thwart this tendency, Temporalist musicians build up during the first twenty years of musical education and practice a vast apperceptual background, so that, ideally, later in their lives, no pulsatory context take them by surprise but, on the contrary, give them a comfortable sensation of *dejà vú*. The consequence of this active perception training is a certain automatization at the level of fast actonic temporal windows successions. The magic of Temporalist music is largely indebted to this particular, acquired ability.

J.-P.: If your own improvisations please you and if you are able to imagine them transposed graphically, you may consider yourself free to probe the world of musical composition. You have listened to our masterpieces enough to be able to steal some of the common compositional techniques. Repetition, variation and contrast do the job equally well in both musical traditions, as you might have noticed. Perhaps functional ambiguity is more present in the world of pulsations than in the sonorous one, and this is why I encourage you to use it to the fullest, as we did in the last centuries. Other techniques, like progressions, are not to be found in our music, but nobody can prevent you from using them along with pulsatory repetitions.

Another interesting subject opened by Jean-Philippe during that morning was that of "false beats" – something that I noticed myself while listening to Temporalist music – but never bothered to place into a theoretical framework. If concepts such as tempo or metrical hierarchization (at the level of pulsations) are not extant in Temporalist music, pulsatory chunks do form and they are marked by accents that may or may not be thesis prosodical values. As most times we actually deal with TH values, these establish a kind of pulse which, although irregular, is still a pulse. In real music, whenever certain pulsatory structures repeat, these "false beats" awaken certain anticipatory perceptual mechanisms. The confirmation or the denial of these anticipations represent an old compositional trick that Jean-Philippe suggested I use to the extent the formal accessibility of my small creative attempts would interest me.

Upon mustering the ways in which, once returned to Paris, I could cure the "withdrawal" produced by the sudden severance of my contact with Temporalist music, my guide recommended that I quickly compose the book, edit it in the following months and keep our long meeting alive as a strange and nice memory. In other words, I should not consider myself the ambassador of the musical world described in this book.

J.-P.: Should you succeed in writing a good book, be sure that there will be enough scholarly musicians placed on positions of administrative, academic or cultural power who will be more than glad to confiscate our theory and put it onto the narrow horizon of their own frustrations. Believe me, you won't desire to play a role in this scenario. If you listen to my advice, a few years after having published the book you will pick it up and be utterly amazed that once you knew all those strange things – and that will make you a happier man.

(Summer of 2008)

The book is not even proofread in its entirety and I already have doubts that I am its author. I look at my own handwriting and have the impression that it silently lies to me. On the other hand, in the months that have passed since my return, I never felt the need to compose music in the Temporalist style. I do not find that strange at all, as I have never been a composer. A few times, though, I tried to improvise in the Temporalist "manner", but stopped after a couple of minutes. My guides would have been appalled by my poor extemporizations. I assume that the feeling of accomplishment that accompanied me while listening to recordings or Temporalist music concerts primarily stemmed from the accuracy of the 50 ms grid, as handled by their interpreters. The fact that this convention is continuously confirmed without any traceable effort, thus transforming it into second nature, is able to create in us the feeling that those people perform a music that is strange, unearthly maybe – but for sure they know very well what they are doing.

As my mouth went dry after so many cigarettes, I opened a bottle of wine, so that the dawn surprised us well intoxicated, yet continuously debating ever more hackneyed ideas (for instance, how it is to be an old lady in Paris). For the sake of those nice Paris times, when Jean-Philippe's life was a varied pretext for another coffee and many additional smokes, my friend started to help himself to my stack of cigarettes (the first ones inhaled into his own lungs). "Horrible", he murmured each time he lit the first ten, after which he started to bum me off directly, tapping his lips with his fingers. A short time after dawn, we were both able to break into a tobacconist shop in order to get a purse of dried tota leaves. Jean-Philippe became tense like a prowling carnivore while scanning the cultivated fields that stretched on either side of the dirt road. Then he halted abruptly, like a sniffing hound that has just sensed the floating molecules of an alluring and vivid smell. In no time, our gig became a vantage point:

– You come with me! Jean-Philippe commanded.

Indeed, two acres from the road, after crossing a little orchard, the scent of a stubble seemed to disperse in the air a familiar smell. The plants had probably been harvested in the fall and all that was left were thousands of stubs, severed some four fingers above the soil. From place to place, one or two long leaves, now dried and soiled, were still attached. Jean-Philippe started to collect them passionately, and in a few minutes he placed in my arms a small sheaf:

– Smokers' solidarity bears no limits! We are so fortunate not to live in your European Union!

As we had had no reason to bring a knife, Jean-Philippe had a brilliant idea as to how should we use those leaves. The driest ones were loosely spiralled around a stick. After removing it, he would hold the 5-6 inch long leaf in his fist, lighting it at one end and inhaling the smoke through the other. As the ember approached his fingers, he would lift them one by one – an excellent survival exercise for a desperate smoker.

After quenching the vice that had stopped us from our trip, I told Jean-Philippe that I wouldn't want to return to Paris before seeing the "plums" that their wine is produced from. For that to happen, we had to go to a nearby farm, as the locals cultivate that plant close to their homes and to a water source. To my surprise, I found out that Temporalist wine is produced from the water deposited inside the subterranean bulbs of a plant that looks from the outside like a giant bull thistle. Like a cactus, during the rainy seasons this vegetable stores an important quantity of water, to be used during the dry days of summer. The farmers know that if the plant is watered during those hot days, the stored liquid becomes a kind of sweet syrup that after a few months may be harvested and placed in fermentation barrels. The seeds of the plant are kept and planted again, for the next crop.

(Summer of 2008)

I decided to keep the last paragraphs and thank the two plants that kept me from spending two years without any of the small pleasures of life which are so important to a Frenchman like myself.

There is an episode that I am unable to place precisely in time, but at some point Jean-Philippe presented me with a list of compositions from Temporalissima's manuscripts collection and asked me to check out about twenty short pieces that I think I could sight-read, should I have a piano at my disposition. After a few weeks, while pacing the alley that linked the diner to the small room that I used to dwell in at that time (that is where I kept my personal items and skirts), I was literally taken aloft by a platoon of bacchanals composed of young professors, students and their respective partners – and hauled into a big chaise. I was immediately taken care of by one of the girls who explained to me that the young boys who were pulling us ahead were just following Jean-Philippe's orders. During the three or four hours spent on the road, I heard a few dozen Temporalist jokes that either outlined a sense of humor that was weirder than a polar parrot or were simply untranslatable by my poor mental representations. The gallivanters, though, were continuously laughing, while the lads were sending me significant glances. Most of them were professors and students from the university to which Jean-Philippe himself was affiliated to at that moment, and that perhaps explains why they knew so many things about me. Or was it the new vice that I had just introduced to his immediate circles of friends and acquaintances? Just a few weeks had passed since I discovered that the tota leaves could be smoked, yet two of the girls and a tall professor who was laughing selectively at the jokes passed around clumsily rolled cigarettes that they then smoked with gusto.

Our destination was a kind of rural dance hall placed at a comfortable distance from a city that I never managed to visit. Inside it, Jean-Philippe and Monique had prepared all the necessary stuff for a small party: snacks, a panoply of musical instruments and lots of wine. Monique was smoking and I deduced from her eyes that she adored me for that, the same way you adore a writer whose prose made you burst into tears or laugh. That was quite understandable as after an accommodation week, during which I tested a dozen blends of tota tea, I managed to find a brand that was not at all peppery, while the smoke was as perfumed as that of the Duch tobacco I myself used to roll in my late teens.

On a small stage there was Temporalissima's piano, obtained after some mischievous maneuvers by some of the students who, one day before, had stuffed the old lady with heavy and abundant foods during a banquet organized after one of her recitals. At the end of the party, the gluttonized pianist felt sick and was immediately transported to a special sanatorium that was far enough away for the culprits to have time to steal the piano, use it for some unorthodox purposes, and put it back in place.

The "sensation" of the evening was… myself, sight-reading the scores piled up on the piano lid in a variety of ordinary tempi (as far as I was concerned) that sounded quite exotic to their ears. Along with the scores that I had checked up a week before and which Jean-Philippe had himself copied on some large sheets of paper, I also found, on the piano, the scores with which Temporalissima traveled during the interrupted tour.

As the wine was intriguingly dry (their wines are usually quite sweet), I started to gorge glass after glass until my fingers ceased obeying my commands. At that point, helped by Jean-Philippe's translation, I asked the musicians to stop admiring my silly tempi, pick up their instruments and try to jam alongside my improvisations.

As my adolescence was marked by my fascination for Scriabin's piano music, I have since developed a remarkable facility for superimposing two or even three types of tuplets of a large beat (IOI 850-1000 ms). I have split the keyboard into three easily discernible registers and started to improvise such superimpositions, changing at times the tempo and encouraging the instrumentalists to ignore the 50 ms "dictatorship" while imitating my odd (to them) IOIs. They also split into a few groups: some were imitating my bass line, others my right hand improvisations while others tried to combine both. They enjoyed the experiment while I promised to myself never to get drunk again in that world where one cannot sleep during a severe hangover.

That happened perhaps some six to eight months before my "farewell week". Back at his home, Jean-Philippe forbade me any ingestion or smoking of tota leaves. As a result I was tormented with a nagging somnolence, while my brain seemed to have forgotten how to press the switch and turn the "lights" off. Meanwhile, Monique asked me for smoking advice. Dozens of questions – which Jean-Philippe could have answered with equal competence, but he only played the role of the translator: what the filters are made of, if it is OK to blow the smoke through your nose, what a cigarette holder was. In a word, I could not wait to get back home and sleep in my own bed for another two years. While feeling like hell, I had to attend "a very special concert organized in the honour of my departure and of the two things that will forever remain in the minds and hearts of my Temporalist friends". That is how formal Jean-Philippe's spoken invitation sounded. Moving like an alcoholic who fears lucidity, I strolled down the forest pathway that led to the concert hall. Inside it there was a fire. At least that is what I assumed after opening the back door. As we entered the corridor, the tota smoke got thicker and thicker, so that once we arrived in the amphitheater we had to make a visual effort in order to keep track of each other.

"My" seat, the very one I originally found my Temporalist arse sitting on, had been transformed into an electric chair. It was surrounded by a number of contraptions provided with belts, while behind it, the only Temporalist with a non-Temporalist look handled the many buttons, levers and handles of a control panel that was supposed, I imagined, to make me burn slowly. "Clara Morgane", who just appeared from the right smoke curtain along with an even more aged Herr Professor, offered me a huge pill and a glass of water, while the venerable psychologist kept shouting:

– Trink, trink, trink!

Once placed in the chair, while I was strapped with belts and fixed electrodes and suction cups, I could finally have a better look over the audience: everybody was smoking, even the children! I wonder what would have happened if, instead of the tota "tobacco", I had reinvented dynamite for these people.

– They are smoking in your honor, Monique whispered while extracting a cold electrode from my left ear.

– They are smoking for you, Jean-Philippe affably translated, though I had already understood, while doing the same thing with the electric file from my right ear.

– Be kalm, be kalm, be kalm! Herr Professor added, knocking on the little tin helmet that he had just placed on my head.

Clara had burst in tears, and that was not at all something to make me remain "kalm". The contraptions placed behind my chair started to go *vuuu...*, and I closed my eyes waiting to either enter a long tunnel or see myself from the ceiling, trembling from all my limbs, having my eyes pop out like exploding popcorn kernels and sticking out my tongue.

Ten, nine, eight, seven... nothing. Six, five... and the stage suddenly got animated. Two men were placing upon it Temporalissima's piano, after which a small orchestra of eight filled the space, one of the instrumentalists taking a seat at the piano. It was not hard to recognize them, as they were all present at that party that taught me never to get drunk again if I could not bargain a few hours of sleep or rest.

After a boring, repetitive speech in which Jean-Philippe announced that in a few minutes I would be dead and famous, I was presented with "a European-style improvisation concert performed by the students of our French guest". My students... no more, no less. I managed to listen to the first few minutes of the concert in which the musicians were lamely trying to recompose our "jam session", after which I felt an urge to run out, faint or die. The smoke already made the air unbreathable while I started to contemplate the cessation of the fatigue (caused by the interruption of tota ingestion) with a self-strangulation. What a pity my hands were immobilized! And as if that were not enough, the pill that I had just swallowed produced a harsh heartburn down my throat, while the mild electrocutions started to make me itch all over my body. If I could only free my hands… I knew what to do with them – I would use one to strangle myself, while with the other I would scratch…

The last image I can remember is that of Clara wiping off her tears, while the Professor kept repeating to me in English, one inch from my nose, that he would send me a letter.

Well, when I receive it, I will know what to do with it. At the moment I am happy that I managed to keep my word given to my guides and reproduce in a book the things that they have taught me. Any other word added here would be superfluous.

(Summer of 2008)

This is the last day of August and the letter promised to me in another world has not as yet reached my postal box. There won't be, therefore, an epilogue to this story.

Marseille, October 28, 2008

Dear Sir,
or
Dear Madam,

My American professor, Mrs. J. D. K., who presently guides my doctoral thesis, asked me to outline a bibliographic list of about fifty authors for the benefit of those who would like to study the ways people relate cognitively to the pulsatory-temporal stimuli during music perception and production.

In the case of certain authors, who published a large number of studies in various places, I preferred to notate the internet page hosting their list of publications.

I also added the websites of the relevant research groups.

After accomplishing this task, Mrs. J. D. K. asked me to send a printed copy of these references to a Paris drugstore.

Hoping that this letter reaches the right person, I send you my professor's "best zeuxilogic regards".

Yours sincerely,
D. E.

167

1. Abravaya, Ido. 2006. *On Bach's rhythm and tempo*. Bochumer Arbeiten zur Musikwissenschaft – Bd. 4, Bärenreiter Hochschulschriften.
2. Berry, Wallace. 1976. *Structural functions of music*. New York: Dover Publications, Inc.
3. Boltz, Marilyn. http://www.haverford.edu/psych/mboltz/
4. Buzsaki, Gyorgy. 2006. *Rhythms of the Brain*. Oxford University Press.
5. Clarke, Eric F. http://www.music.ox.ac.uk/people/staff-listings/academics/e_clarke/publications1.html
6. Clynes, Manfred. 1977. *Sentics: The touch of emotions*. Bridport, Dorset: Prism Press.
   http://www.microsoundmusic.com/bibliography.html?bpid=8882
7. Cooper, Grosvenor, Leonard B. Meyer. 1960. *The rhythmic structure of music*. Chicago: University of Chicago Press.
8. Desain, Peter. http://www.nici.kun.nl/mmm/
9. Deutsch, Diana, ed. 1982. *The psychology of music*. New York: Academic Press.
10. Drake, Carolyn. http://www.biomedexperts.com/Profile.bme/341000/Carolyn_Drake
11. Eck, Douglas. http://www.iro.umontreal.ca/~eckdoug/publications.html
12. Epstein, David. 1995. *Shaping time: Music, the brain, and performance*. New York: Schrimer Books.
13. Evans, James R., Manfred Clynes. 1986. *Rhythm in psychological, linguistic and musical processes*. Springfield, Illinois: Charles C. Thomas Publisher.
14. Fraisse, Paul. 1964. *The psychology of time*. London: Eyre & Spottiswoode.
15. Friberg, Anders. http://www.speech.kth.se/staff/homepage/index.html?id=afriberg
16. Gillingham, Bryan. 1986. *Modal rhythm. Musicological studies*, vol. XLVI. Ottawa: The institute of Mediaeval music.
17. Grondin, Simon, ed. 2008. *Psychology of time*. Emerald Group Publishing Ltd.
18. Hoerl, Christoph, Teresa McCormack, eds. 2001. *Time and memory: Issues in philosophy and psychology* (Consciousness and self-consciousness series, 1). Oxford University Press
19. Honing, Henkjan. http://cf.hum.uva.nl/mmm/index.html?personal/honing.html&target
20. Huron, David. 2008. *Sweet anticipation: Music and the psychology of expectation*. The MIT Press.

21. Jones, Mari Riess. http://labs.psy.ohio-state.edu/roar/mari_jones. html

22. Kramer, Jonathan D. 1988. *The time of music: New meanings, new temporalities, new listening strategies*. New York: Schrimer Books.

23. Kramer, Jonathan D., ed. 1993. *Time in contemporary musical thought*. Contemporary music review series. Vol. 7, Part 2. Harwood Academic Publishers GmbH.

24. Lerdahl, Fred, Ray Jackendoff. 1996. *A generative theory of tonal music*. The MIT Press.

25. Levitin, Daniel J. *This is your brain on music. The science of a human obsession*. New York: Dutton Adult (Penguin), 2006

26. London, Justin. 2004. *Hearing in time: Psychological aspects of musical meter*. Oxford University Press. http://www.people.carleton.edu/~jlondon/j._london_curriculum_vitae.htm

27. Madison, Guy. 2001. *Functional modelling of the human timing mechanism*. Uppsala: Acta universitatis Upsaliensis. http://www.psy.umu.se/om-institutionen/personal/guy-madison

28. Marsden, Alan. 2000. *Representing musical time: A temporal-logic approach*. Studies on new music research series. Lisse: Swets & Zeitlinger.

29. Meyer, Leonard B. 1956. *Emotion and meaning in music*. The University of Chicago Press.

30. Michon, John A. http://www.jamichon.nl/jam_writings/jam_writings_time.htm

31. Moelants, Dirk. http://www.ipem.ugent.be/?q=user/4

32. Music, Mind, Machine Group (MMMG): http://www.nici.kun.nl/mmm/

33. Nakajima, Yoshitaka. http://www.kyushu-id.ac.jp/~ynhome/ENG/Research/index.html

34. Ornstein, Robert E. 1970. *On the experience of time*. Harmondsworth Middlesex: Penguin Books Ltd.

35. Palmer, Caroline. http://www.mcgill.ca/spl/publications/

36. Parasuraman, Raja, ed. 2000. *The Attentive Brain*. The MIT Press.

37. Pashler, Harold, ed. 1998. *Attention*. Studies in cognition series. Psychology Press.

38. Povel, Dirk-Jan. http://www.socsci.kun.nl/~povel/Publications/Index.html

39. Pöppel, Ernst. 1988. *Mindworks: Time and conscious experience*. Orlando, Florida: Harcourt Brace Jovanovich, Publishers.

40. Reiner, Thomas. 2000. *Semiotics of musical time*. Berkeley insights in linguistics and semiotics, vol. 43. New York: Peter Lang Publishing, Inc.

41. Repp, Bruno. http://www.haskins.yale.edu/staff/repp.html

42. Rhythm Perception and Production Workshop (RPPW): http://rppw.org/
https://mercure.iro.umontreal.ca/pipermail/rppw/
http://www.nici.kun.nl/mmm/rppw/program.html
http://cspeech.ucd.ie/~rppw/rppw10/

43. Sacks, Oliver. 2008. *Musicophilia: Tales of music and the brain*. Vintage Books Publishers.

44. Sethares, William A. 2007. *Rhythm and transforms*. London: Springer-Verlag.

45. Shapiro, Kimron, ed. 2001. *The limits of attention: Temporal constraints on human information processing*. Oxford University Press.

46. Swain, Joseph P. 2002. *Harmonic rhythm: Analysis and interpretation*. Oxford University Press.

47. Thaut, Michael. 2005. *Rhythm, music, and the brain: Scientific foundations and clinical applications*. Studies on new music research series. Routledge Publishers.

48. van Noorden, Leon. http://www.ipem.ugent.be/?q=user/8

49. Volk, Anja. http://people.cs.uu.nl/volk/

50. Vorberg, Dirk. http://en.scientificcommons.org/dirk_vorberg

51. Windsor, Luke, Peter Desain, ed. 2000. *Rhythm: Perception and production*. Studies on new music research series. Lisse: Swets & Zeitlinger.

52. Windsor, Luke. http://www.leeds.ac.uk/music/staff/lw/

53. Wohlschläger, Andreas. http://en.scientificcommons.org/andreas_wohlschläger

CONTENTS

64351288R00097

Made in the USA
Middletown, DE
12 February 2018